DEAD MAN'S PLACK

MORE WILDSIDE CLASSICS

Dacobra, or The White Priests of Ahriman, by Harris Burland
The Nabob, by Alphonse Daudet
Out of the Wreck, by Captain A. E. Dingle
The Elm-Tree on the Mall, by Anatole France
The Lance of Kanana, by Harry W. French
Amazon Nights, by Arthur O. Friel
Caught in the Net, by Emile Gaboriau
The Gentle Grafter, by O. Henry
Raffles, by E. W. Hornung
Gates of Empire, by Robert E. Howard
Tom Brown's School Days, by Thomas Hughes
The Opium Ship, by H. Bedford Jones
The Miracles of Antichrist, by Selma Lagerlof
Arsène Lupin, by Maurice LeBlanc
A Phantom Lover, by Vernon Lee
The Iron Heel, by Jack London
The Witness for the Defence, by A.E.W. Mason
The Spider Strain and Other Tales, by Johnston McCulley
Tales of Thubway Tham, by Johnston McCulley
The Prince of Graustark, by George McCutcheon
Bull-Dog Drummond, by Cyril McNeile
The Moon Pool, by A. Merritt
The Red House Mystery, by A. A. Milne
Blix, by Frank Norris
Wings over Tomorrow, by Philip Francis Nowlan
The Devil's Paw, by E. Phillips Oppenheim
Satan's Daughter and Other Tales, by E. Hoffmann Price
The Insidious Dr. Fu Manchu, by Sax Rohmer
Mauprat, by George Sand
The Slayer and Other Tales, by H. de Vere Stacpoole
Penrod (Gordon Grant Illustrated Edition), by Booth Tarkington
The Gilded Age, by Mark Twain
The Blockade Runners, by Jules Verne
The Gadfly, by E.L. Voynich

Please see www.wildsidepress.com for a complete list!

DEAD MAN'S PLACK

W. H. HUDSON

WILDSIDE PRESS

DEAD MAN'S PLACK

This edition published in 2006 by Wildside Press, LLC.
www.wildsidepress.com

CONTENTS

DEAD MAN'S PLACK. 7

AN OLD THORN. 87

POSTSCRIPT. 111

DEAD MAN'S PLACK

PREAMBLE

"The insect tribes of human kind" is a mode of expression we are familiar with in the poets, moralists and other superior persons, or beings, who viewing mankind from their own vast elevation see us all more or less of one size and very, very small. No doubt the comparison dates back to early, probably Pliocene, times, when some one climbed to the summit of a very tall cliff, and looking down and seeing his fellows so diminished in size as to resemble insects, not so gross as beetles perhaps but rather like emmets, he laughed in the way they laughed then at the enormous difference between his stature and theirs. Hence the time-honoured and serviceable metaphor.

Now with me, in this particular instance, it was all the other way about — from insect to man — seeing that it was when occupied in watching the small comedies and tragedies of the insect world on its stage that I stumbled by chance upon a compelling reminder of one of the greatest tragedies in England's history — greatest, that is to say, in its consequences. And this is how it happened.

One summer day, prowling in an extensive oak wood, in Hampshire, known as Harewood Forest, I discovered that it counted among its inhabitants no fewer than three species of insects of peculiar interest to me, and from that time I haunted it, going there day after day to spend long hours in pursuit of my small quarry. Not to kill and preserve their diminutive corpses in a cabinet, but solely to witness the comedy of their brilliant little lives. And as I used to take my luncheon in my pocket I fell into the habit of going to a particular spot, some opening in the dense wood with a big tree to lean against and give me shade, where after refreshing myself with food and drink I could smoke my pipe in solitude and peace. Eventually I came to prefer one spot for my midday rest in the central part of the wood, where a stone cross, slender, beautifully proportioned and about eighteen feet high, had been erected some seventy or eighty years before by the lord of the manor. On one side of the great stone block on which the cross stood there was an inscription which told that it was placed there to mark the spot known from of old as Dead Man's Plack; that, according to tradition, handed from father to son, it was just here that King Edgar slew his friend and favourite Earl Athelwold, when hunting in the forest.

I had sat there on many occasions, and had glanced from time to time at the inscription cut on the stone, once actually reading it, without having my attention drawn away from the insect world I was living in. It was not the tradition of the Saxon king nor the beauty of the cross in that green wilderness which drew me daily to the spot, but its solitariness and the little open space where I could sit in the shade and have my rest.

Then something happened. Some friends from town came down to me at the hamlet I was staying at, and one of the party, the mother of most of them, was not only older than the rest of us in years, but also in knowledge and wisdom; and at the same time she was younger than the youngest of us, since she had the curious mind, the undying interest in everything on earth — the secret, in fact, of everlasting youth. Naturally, being of this temperament, she wanted to know what I was doing and all about what I had seen, even to the minutest detail — the smallest insect — and in telling her of my days I spoke casually of the cross placed at a spot called Dead Man's Plack. This at once reminded her of something she had heard about it before, but long ago, in the seventies of last century; then presently it all came back to her, and it proved to me an interesting story.

It chanced that in that far back time she was in correspondence on certain scientific and literary subjects with a gentleman who was a native of this part of Hampshire in which we were staying, and that they got into a discussion about Freeman, the historian, during which he told her of an incident of his undergraduate days when Freeman was professor at Oxford. He attended a lecture by that man on the Mythical and Romantic Elements in Early English History, in which he stated for the guidance of all who study the past, that they must always bear in mind the inevitable passion for romance in men, especially the uneducated, and that when the student comes upon a romantic incident in early history, even when it accords with the known character of the person it relates to, he must reject it as false. Then, to rub the lesson in, he gave an account of the most flagrant of the romantic lies contained in the history of the Saxon kings. This was the story of King Edgar, and how his favourite, Earl Athelwold, deceived him as to the reputed beauty of Elfrida, and how Edgar in revenge slew Athelwold with his own hand when hunting. Then — to show how false it all was! — Edgar, the chronicles state, was at Salisbury and rode in one day to Harewood Forest and there slew Athelwold. Now, said Freeman, as Harewood Forest is in Yorkshire, Edgar could not have ridden there from Salisbury in one day, nor in two, nor in three, which was enough to show that the whole story was a fabrication.

The undergraduate, listening to the lecturer, thought the Professor was wrong owing to his ignorance of the fact that the Harewood Forest in which the deed was done was in Hampshire, within a day's ride from Salisbury, and that local tradition points to the very spot in the forest where Athelwold was slain. Accordingly he wrote to the Professor and gave him these facts. His letter was not answered; and the poor youth felt hurt, as he thought he was doing Professor Freeman a service by telling him something he didn't know. *He* didn't know his Professor Freeman.

This story about Freeman tickled me, because I dislike him, but if any one were to ask me why I dislike him I should probably have to answer like a woman: Because I do. Or if stretched on the rack until I could find or invent a better reason I should perhaps say it was because he was so infernally cock-sure, so convinced that he and he alone had the power of distinguishing between the true and false; also that he was so arbitrary and arrogant and ready to trample on those who doubted his infallibility.

All this, I confess, would not be much to say against him, seeing that it is nothing but the ordinary professorial or academic mind, and I suppose that the only difference between Freeman and the ruck of the professors was that he was more impulsive or articulate and had a greater facility in expressing his scorn.

Here I may mention in passing that when this lecture appeared in print in his *Historical Essays* he had evidently been put out a little, and also put on his mettle by that letter from an undergraduate, and had gone more deeply into the documents relating to the incident, seeing that he now relied mainly on the discrepancies in half a dozen chronicles he was able to point out to prove its falsity. His former main argument now appeared as a "small matter of detail" — a "confusion of geography" in the different versions of the old historians. But one tells us, Freeman writes, that Athelwold was killed in the Forest of Wherwell on his way to York, and then he says: "Now as Wherwell is in Hampshire, it could not be on the road to York;" and further on he says: "Now Harewood Forest in Yorkshire is certainly not the same as Wherwell in Hampshire," and so on, and on, and on, but always careful not to say that Wherwell Forest and Harewood Forest are two names for one and the same place, although now the name of Wherwell is confined to the village on the Test, where it is supposed

Athelwold had his castle and lived with his wife before he was killed, and where Elfrida in her declining years, when trying to make her peace with God, came and built a Priory and took the habit herself and there finished her darkened life.

This then was how he juggled with words and documents and chronicles (his thimble-rigging), making a truth a lie or a lie a truth according as it suited a froward and prejudicate mind, to quote the expression of an older and simpler-minded historian — Sir Walter Raleigh.

Finally, to wind up the whole controversy, he says you are to take it as a positive truth that Edgar married Elfrida, and a positive falsehood that Edgar killed Athelwold. Why — seeing there is as good authority and reason for believing the one statement as the other? A foolish question! Why? — Because I, Professor or Pope Freeman, say so!

The main thing here is the effect the Freeman anecdote had on me, which was that when I went back to continue my insect-watching and rested at noon at Dead Man's Plack, the old legend would keep intruding itself on my mind, until, wishing to have done with it, I said and I swore that it was true — that the tradition preserved in the neighbourhood, that on this very spot Athelwold was slain by the king, was better than any document or history. It was an act which had been witnessed by many persons, and the memory of it preserved and handed down from father to son for thirty generations; for it must be borne in mind that the inhabitants of this district of Andover and the villages on the Test have never in the last thousand years been exterminated or expelled. And ten centuries is not so long for an event of so startling a character to persist in the memory of the people when we consider that such traditions have come down to us even from prehistoric times and have proved true. Our archæologists, for example, after long study of the remains, cannot tell us how long ago — centuries or thousands of years — a warrior with golden armour was buried under the great cairn at Mold in Flintshire.

And now the curious part of all this matter comes in. Having taken my side in the controversy and made my pronouncement, I found that I was not yet free of it. It remained with me, but in a new way — not as an old story in old books, but as an event, or series of events, now being re-enacted before my very eyes. I actually saw and heard it all, from the very beginning to the dreadful end; and this is what I am now going to relate. But whether or not I shall in my relation be in close accord with what history tells us I know not, nor does it matter in the least. For just as the religious mystic is exempt from the study of theology and the whole body of religious doctrine, and from all the observances necessary to those who in fear and trembling are seeking their salvation, even so those who have been brought to the *Gate of Remembrance* are independent of written documents, chronicles and histories, and of the weary task of separating the false from the true. They have better sources of information. For I am not so vain as to imagine for one moment that without such external aid I am able to make shadows breathe, revive the dead, and know what silent mouths once said.

I

When, sitting at noon in the shade of an oak tree at Dead Man's Plack, I beheld Edgar, I almost ceased to wonder at the miracle that had happened in this war-mad, desolated England, where Saxon and Dane, like two infuriated bull-dogs, were everlastingly at grips, striving to tear each other's throats out, and deluging the country with blood; how, ceasing from their strife, they had all at once agreed to live in peace and unity side by side under the young king; and this seemingly unnatural state of things endured even to the end of his life, on which account he was called Edgar the Peaceful.

He was beautiful in person and had infinite charm, and these gifts, together with his kingly qualities, which have won the admiration of all men of all ages, endeared him to his people. He was but thirteen when he came to be king of united England, and small for his age, but even in these terrible times he was remarkable for his courage, both physical and moral. Withal he had a subtle mind; indeed, I think he surpassed all our kings of the past thousand years in combining so many excellent qualities. His was the wisdom of the serpent combined with the gentleness — I will not say of the dove, but rather of the cat, our little tiger on the hearthrug, the most beautiful of four-footed things, so lithe, so soft, of so affectionate a disposition, yet capable when suddenly roused to anger of striking with lightning rapidity and rending the offender's flesh with its cruel, unsheathed claws.

Consider the line he took, even as a boy! He recognised among all those who surrounded him, in his priestly adviser, the one man of so great a mind as to be capable of assisting him effectually in ruling so divided, war-loving and revengeful a people, and he allowed him practically unlimited power to do as he liked. He went even further by pretending to fall in with Dunstan's ambitions of purging the Church of the order of priests or half-priests, or canons, who were in possession of most of the religious houses in England, and were priests that married wives and owned lands and had great power. Against this monstrous state of things Edgar rose up in his simulated wrath and cried out to Archbishop Dunstan in a speech he delivered to sweep them away and purify the Church and country from such a scandal!

But Edgar himself had a volcanic heart, and to witness it in full eruption it was only necessary to convey to him the tidings of some woman of a rare loveliness; and have her he would, in spite of all laws human and divine. Thus when inflamed with passion for a beautiful nun he did not hesitate to smash the gates of a convent to drag her forth and forcibly make her his mistress. And this too was a dreadful scandal, but no great pother could be made about it, seeing that Edgar was so powerful a friend of the Church and of pure religion.

Now all the foregoing is contained in the histories, but in what follows I have for sole light and guide the vision that came to me at Dead Man's Plack, and have only to add to this introductory note that Edgar at the early age of twenty-two was a widower, having already had to wife Ethelfled the Fair, who was famous for her beauty, and who died shortly after giving birth to a child who lived to figure later in history as one of England's many Edwards.

II

Now although King Edgar had dearly loved his wife, who was also beloved by all his people on account of her sweet and gentle disposition as well as of her exceeding beauty, it was not in his nature to brood long over such a loss. He had too keen a zest for life and the many interests and pleasures it had for him ever to become a melancholy man. It was a delight to him to be king, and to perform all kingly duties and offices. Also he was happy in his friends, especially in his favourite, the Earl Athelwold, who was like him in character, a man after his own heart. They were indeed like brothers, and some of those who surrounded the king were not too well pleased to witness this close intimacy. Both were handsome men, witty, of a genial disposition, yet under a light careless manner brave and ardent, devoted to the pleasure of the chase and all other pleasures, especially to those bestowed by golden Aphrodite, their chosen saint, albeit her name did not figure in the Calendar.

Hence it was not strange, when certain reports of the wonderful beauty of a woman in the West Country were brought to Edgar's ears that his heart began to burn within him, and that by and by he opened himself to his friend on the subject. He told Athelwold that he had discovered the one woman in England fit to be Ethelfled's successor, and that he had resolved to make her his queen although he had never seen her, since she and her father had never been to court. That, however, would not deter him; there was no other woman in the land whose claims were equal to hers, seeing that she was the only daughter and part heiress of one of the greatest men in the kingdom, Ongar, Earldoman of Devon and Somerset, a man of vast possessions and great power. Yet all that was of less account to him than her fame, her personal worth, since she was reputed to be the most beautiful woman in the land. It was for her beauty that he desired her, and being of an exceedingly impatient temper in any case in which beauty in a woman was concerned, he desired his friend to proceed at once to Earl Ongar in Devon with an offer of marriage to his daughter, Elfrida, from the king.

Athelwold laughed at Edgar in this his most solemn and kingly mood, and with a friend's privilege told him not to be so simple as to buy a pig in a poke. The lady, he said, had not been to court, consequently she had not been seen by those best able to judge of her reputed beauty. Her fame rested wholly on the report of the people of her own country, who were great as every one knew at blowing their own trumpets. Their red and green county was England's paradise; their men the bravest and handsomest and their women the most beautiful in the land. For his part he believed there were as good men and as fair women in Mercia and East Anglia as in the West. It would certainly be an awkward business if the king found himself bound in honour to wed with a person he did not like. Awkward because of her father's fierce pride and power. A better plan would be to send some one he could trust not to make a mistake to find out the truth of the report.

Edgar was pleased at his friend's wise caution, and praised him for his candour, which was that of a true friend, and as he was the only man he could thoroughly trust in such a matter he would send him. Accordingly, Athelwold, still much amused at Edgar's sudden wish to make an offer of marriage to a woman he had never seen, set out on his journey in great state with many attendants as befitted his person and his mission, which was ostensibly to bear greetings and loving messages from the king to some of his most important subjects in the West Country.

In this way he travelled through Wilts, Somerset and

Devon, and in due time arrived at Earl Ongar's castle on the Exe.

III

Athelwold, who thought highly of himself, had undertaken his mission with a light heart, but now when his progress in the West had brought him to the great earldoman's castle it was borne in on him that he had put himself in a very responsible position. He was here to look at this woman with cold, critical eyes, which was easy enough; and having looked at and measured and weighed her, he would make a true report to Edgar; that too would be easy for him, since all his power and happiness in life depended on the king's continual favour. But Ongar stood between him and the woman he had come to see and take stock of with that clear unbiassed judgment which he could safely rely on. And Ongar was a proud and stern old man, jealous of his great position, who had not hesitated to say on Edgar's accession to the kingship, knowing well that his words would be reported in due time, that he refused to be one of the crowd who came flocking from all over the land to pay homage to a boy. It thus came about that neither then nor at any subsequent period had there been any personal relations between the king and this English subject, who was prouder than all the Welsh kings who had rushed at Edgar's call to make their submission.

But now when Ongar had been informed that the king's intimate friend and confidant was on his way to him with greetings and loving messages from Edgar, he was flattered, and resolved to receive him in a friendly and loyal spirit and do him all the honour in his power. For Edgar was no longer a boy: he was king over all this hitherto turbulent realm, East and West from sea to sea and from the Land's End to the Tweed, and the strange enduring peace of the times was a proof of his power.

It thus came to pass that Athelwold's mission was made smooth to him, and when they met and conversed, the fierce old Earl was so well pleased with his visitor, that all trace of the sullen hostility he had cherished towards the court passed away like the shadow of a cloud. And later, in the banqueting-room, Athelwold came face to face with the woman he had come to look at with cold, critical eyes, like one who examines a horse in the interests of a friend who desires to become its purchaser.

Down to that fatal moment the one desire of his heart was to serve his friend faithfully in this delicate business. Now, the first sight of her, the first touch of her hand, wrought a change in him, and all thought of Edgar and of the purpose of his visit vanished out of his mind. Even he, one of the great nobles of his time, the accomplished courtier and life of the court, stood silent like a person spellbound before this woman who had been to no court, but had lived always with that sullen old man in comparative seclusion in a remote province. It was not only the beautiful dignity and graciousness with which she received him, with the exquisite beauty in the lines and colour of her face, and her hair which, if unloosed, would have covered her to the knees as with a splendid mantle. That hair of a colour comparable only to that of the sweet gale when that sweet plant is in its golden withy or catkin stage in the month of May, and is clothed with catkins as with a foliage of a deep shining red gold, that seems not a colour of earth but rather one distilled from the sun itself. Nor was it the colour of her eyes, the deep pure blue of the lungwort, that blue loveliness seen in no other flower on earth. Rather it was the light from her eyes which was like lightning that pierced and startled him; for that light, that expression, was a living spirit looking through his eyes into the depths of his soul, knowing all its strength and weakness, and in the same instant resolving to make it her own and have dominion over it.

It was only when he had escaped from the power and magic of her presence, when alone in his sleeping room, that reflection came to him and the recollection of Edgar and of his mission. And there was dismay in the thought. For the woman was his, part and parcel of his heart and soul and life; for that was what her lightning glance had said to him, and she could not be given to another. No, not to the king! Had any man, any friend, ever been placed in so terrible a position? Honour? Loyalty? To whichever side he inclined he could not escape the crime, the base betrayal and abandonment! But loyalty to the king would be the greater crime. Had not Edgar himself broken every law of God and man to gratify his passion for a woman? Not a woman like this! Never would Edgar look on her until he, Athelwold, had obeyed her and his own heart and made her his for ever! And what would come then! He would not consider it — he would perish rather than yield her to another!

That was how the question came before him, and how it was settled, during the long sleepless hours when his blood was in a fever and his brain on fire; but when day dawned and his blood grew cold and his brain was tired, the image of Edgar betrayed and in a deadly rage became insistent, and he rose desponding and in dread of the meeting to come. And no sooner did he meet her than she overcame him as on the previous day; and so it continued during the whole period of his visit, racked with passion, drawn now to this side, now to that, and when he was most resolved to have her then most furiously assaulted by loyalty, by friendship, by honour, and he was like a stag at bay fighting for his life against the hounds. And every time he met her — and the passionate words he dared not speak were like confined fire, burning him up inwardly — seeing him pale and troubled she would greet him with a smile and look which told him she knew that he was troubled in heart, that a great conflict was raging in him, also that it was on her account and was perhaps because he had already bound himself to some other woman, some great lady of the land; and now this new passion had come to him. And her smile and look were like the world-irradiating sun when it rises, and the black menacing cloud that brooded over his soul would fade and vanish, and he knew that she had again claimed him and that he was hers.

So it continued till the very moment of parting, and again as on their first meeting he stood silent and troubled before her; then in faltering words told her that the thought of her would travel and be with him; that in a little while, perhaps in a month or two, he would be rid of a great matter which had been weighing heavily on his mind, and once free he could return to Devon, if she would consent to his paying her another visit.

She replied smilingly with gracious words, with no change from that exquisite perfect dignity which was always hers; nor tremor in her speech, but only that understanding look from her eyes, which said: Yes, you shall come back to me in good time, when you have smoothed the way, to claim me for your own.

IV

On Athelwold's return the king embraced him warmly, and was quick to observe a change in him — the thinner, paler face and appearance generally of one lately recovered from a grievous illness or who had been troubled in mind. Athelwold explained that it had been a painful visit to him, due in the first place to the anxiety he experienced of being placed in so responsible a position, and in the second place the misery it was to him to be the guest for many days of such a person as the earldoman, a man of a rough, harsh aspect and manner, who daily made himself drunk at table, after which he would grow intolerably garrulous and boastful. Then, when his host had been carried to bed by his servants, his own wakeful, troubled hours would begin. For at first he had been struck by the woman's fine, handsome presence, albeit she was not the peerless beauty she had been reported; but when he had seen her often and more closely and had conversed with her he had been disappointed. There was something lacking; she had not the softness, the charm, desirable in a woman; she had something of her parent's harshness, and his final judgment was that she was not a suitable person for the king to marry.

Edgar was a little cast down at first, but quickly recovering his genial manner, thanked his friend for having served him so well.

For several weeks following the king and the king's favourite were constantly together; and during that period Athelwold developed a peculiar sweetness and affection towards Edgar, often recalling to him their happy boyhood's days in East Anglia, when they were like brothers, and cemented the close friendship which was to last them for the whole of their lives. Finally, when it seemed to his watchful, crafty mind that Edgar had cast the whole subject of his wish to marry Elfrida into oblivion, and that the time was now ripe for carrying out his own scheme, he reopened the subject, and said that although the lady was not a suitable person to be the king's wife it would be good policy on his, Athelwold's, part, to win her on account of her position as only daughter and part heiress of Ongar, who had great power and possessions in the West. But he would not move in the matter without Edgar's consent.

Edgar, ever ready to do anything to please his friend, freely gave it, and only asked him to give an assurance that the secret object of his former visit to Devon would remain inviolate. Accordingly Athelwold took a solemn oath that it would never be revealed, and Edgar then slapped him on the back and wished him Godspeed in his wooing.

Very soon after thus smoothing the way, Athelwold returned to Devon, and was once more in the presence of the woman who had so enchanted him, with that same meaning smile on her lips and light in her eyes which had been her good-bye and her greeting, only now it said to him: You have returned as I knew you would, and I am ready to give myself to you.

From every point of view it was a suitable union, seeing that Athelwold would inherit power and great possessions from his father, Earldoman of East Anglia, and before long the marriage took place, and by and by Athelwold took his wife to Wessex, to the castle he had built for himself on his estate of Wherwell, on the Test. There they lived together, and as they had married for love they were happy.

But as the king's intimate friend and the companion of many of his frequent journeys he could not always bide with her nor be with her for any great length of time. For Edgar had a restless spirit and was exceedingly vigilant, and liked to keep a watchful eye on the different lately hostile nations of Mercia, East Anglia, and Northumbria, so that his journeys were frequent and long to these distant parts of his kingdom. And he also had his naval forces to inspect at frequent intervals. Thus it came about that he was often absent from her for weeks and months at a stretch. And so the time went on, and during these long absences a change would come over Elfrida; the lovely colour, the enchanting smile, the light of her eyes — the outward sign of an intense brilliant life — would fade, and with eyes cast down she would pace the floors or the paths or sit brooding in silence by the hour.

Of all this Athelwold knew nothing, since she made no complaint, and when he returned to her the light and life and brilliance would be hers again, and there was no cloud or shadow on his delight. But the cloud would come back over her when he again went away. Her only relief in her condition was to sit before a fire or when out of doors to seat herself on the bank of the stream and watch the current. For although it was still summer, the month being August, she would have a fire of logs lighted in a large chamber and sit staring at the flames by the hour, and sometimes holding her outstretched hands before the flames until they were hot, she would then press them to her lips. Or when the day was warm and bright she would be out of doors and spend hours by the river gazing at the swift crystal current below as if fascinated by the sight of the running water. It is a marvellously clear water, so that looking down on it you can see the rounded pebbles in all their various colours and markings lying at the bottom, and if there should be a trout lying there facing the current and slowly waving his tail from side to side, you could count the red spots on his side, so clear is the water. Even more did the floating water-grass hold her gaze — that bright green grass that, rooted in the bed of the stream, sends its thin blades to the surface where they float and wave like green floating hair. Stooping, she would dip a hand in the stream and watch the bright clear water running through the fingers of her white hand, then press the hand to her lips.

Then again when day declined she would quit the stream to sit before the blazing logs, staring at the flames. What am I doing here? she would murmur. And what is this my life? When I was at home in Devon I had a dream of Winchester, of Salisbury, or other great towns further away, where the men and women who are great in the land meet together, and where my eyes would perchance sometimes have the happiness to behold the king himself — my husband's close friend and companion. My waking has brought a different scene before me; this castle in the wilderness, a solitude where from an upper window I look upon leagues of forest, a haunt of wild animals. I see great birds soaring in the sky and listen to the shrill screams of kite and buzzard; and sometimes when lying awake on a still night the distant long howl of a wolf. Also, it is said, there are great stags, and roe-deer, and wild boars, and it is Athelwold's joy to hunt them and slay them with his spear. A joy too when he returns from the hunt or from a long absence to play with his beautiful wife — his caged bird of pretty feathers and a sweet song to soothe him when he is tired. But of his life at court he tells me little, and of even that little I doubt the truth. Then he leaves me and I am alone with his retainers — the crowd of serving men and women and the armed men to safeguard me. I am alone with my two friends which I have found, one out of doors, the other in — the river which runs at the bottom of the ground where I take my walks, and the fire I sit before. The two friends, companions, and lovers to whom all the secrets of my soul are confided. I love them, having no other in the world to love, and here I hold my hands before the flames until it is hot and then kiss the heat, and by the stream I kiss my wetted hands. And if I were to remain here until this life became unendurable I should consider as to which one of these two lovers I should give myself. This one I think is too ardent in his love — it would be terrible to be wrapped round in his fiery arms and feel his fiery mouth on mine. I should rather go to the other one to lie down on his pebbly bed, and give myself to him to hold me in his cool, shining arms and mix his green hair with my loosened hair. But my wish is to live and not die. Let me then wait a little longer; let me watch and listen, and perhaps some day, by and by, from his own lips, I shall capture the secret of this my caged solitary life.

And the very next day Athelwold, having just returned with the king to Salisbury, was once more with her; and the brooding cloud had vanished from her life and countenance; she was once more his passionate bride, lavishing caresses on him, listening with childish delight to every word that fell from his lips, and desiring no other life and no greater happiness than this.

V

It was early September, and the king with some of the nobles who were with him, after hunting the deer over against Cranbourne, returned at evening to Salisbury, and after meat with some of his intimates they sat late drinking wine and fell into a merry, boisterous mood. They spoke of Athelwold, who was not with them, and indulged in some mocking remarks about his frequent and prolonged absences from the king's company. Edgar took it in good part and smilingly replied that it had been reported to him that the earl was now wedded to a woman with a will. Also he knew that her father, the great Earldoman of Devon, had been famed for his tremendous physical strength. It was related of him that he had once been charged by a furious bull, that he had calmly waited the onset and had dealt the animal a staggering blow with his fist on its head and had then taken it up in his arms and hurled it into the river Exe. If, he concluded, the daughter had inherited something of this power it was not to be wondered at that she was able to detain her husband at home.

Loud laughter followed this pleasantry of the king's, then one of the company remarked that not a woman's will, though it might be like steel of the finest temper, nor her muscular power, would serve to change Athelwold's nature or keep him from his friend, but only a woman's exceeding beauty.

Then Edgar, seeing that he had been put upon the defence of his absent friend, and that all of them were eager to hear his next word, replied that there was no possession a man was prouder of than that of a beautiful wife; that it was more to him than his own best qualities, his greatest actions, or than titles and lands and gold. If Athelwold had indeed been so happy as to secure the most beautiful woman he would have been glad to bring her to court to exhibit her to all — friends and foes alike — for his own satisfaction and glory.

Again they greeted his speech with laughter, and one cried out: Do you believe it?

Then another, bolder still, exclaimed: It's God's truth that she is the fairest woman in the land — perhaps no fairer has been in any land since Helen of Troy. This I can swear to, he added, smiting the board with his hand, because I have it from one who saw her at her home in Devon before her marriage. One who is a better judge in such matters than I am or than any one at this table, not excepting the king, seeing that he is not only gifted with the serpent's wisdom but with that creature's cold blood as well.

Edgar heard him frowningly, then ended the discussion by rising, and silence fell on the company, for all saw that he was offended. But he was not offended with them, since they knew nothing of his and Athelwold's secret, and what they thought and felt about his friend was nothing to him. But these fatal words about Elfrida's beauty had pierced him with a sudden suspicion of his friend's treachery. And Athelwold was the man he greatly loved — the companion of all his years since their boyhood together. Had he betrayed him in this monstrous way — wounding him in his tenderest part? The very thought that such a thing might be was like a madness in him. Then he reflected — then he remembered, and said to himself: Yes, let me follow his teaching in this matter too, as in the other, and exercise caution and look before I leap. I shall look and look well and see and judge for myself.

The result was that when his boon companions next met him there was no shadow of displeasure in him; he was in a peculiarly genial mood, and so continued. And when his friend returned he embraced him and gently upbraided him for having kept away for so long a time. He begged him to remember that he was his one friend and confidant who was more than a brother to him, and that if wholly deprived of his company he would regard himself as the loneliest man in the kingdom. Then in a short time he spoke once more in the same strain, and said he had not yet sufficiently honoured his friend before the world, and that he proposed visiting him at his own castle to make the acquaintance of his wife and spend a day with him hunting the boar in Harewood Forest.

Athelwold, secretly alarmed, made a suitable reply, expressing his delight at the prospect of receiving the king, and begging him to give him a couple of days' notice before making his visit, so as to give him time to make all preparation for his entertainment.

This the king promised, and also said that this would be an informal visit to a friend, that he would go alone with some of his servants and huntsmen and ride there one day, hunt the next day and return to Salisbury on the third day. And a little later, when the day of his visit was fixed on, Athelwold returned in haste with an anxious mind to his castle.

Now his hard task and the most painful moment of his life had come. Alone with Elfrida in her chamber he cast himself down before her, and with his bowed head resting on her knees, made a clean breast of the whole damning story of the deceit he had practised towards the king in order to win her for himself. In anguish and shedding tears he implored her forgiveness, begging her to think of that irresistible power of love she had inspired in him, which would have made it worse than death to see her the wife of another — even of Edgar himself — his friend, the brother of his soul. Then he went on to speak of Edgar, who was of a sweet and lovable nature, yet capable of a deadly fury against those who offended him; and this was an offence he would take more to heart than any other; he would be implacable if he once thought that he had been wilfully deceived, and she only could now save them from certain destruction. For now it seemed to him that Edgar had conceived a suspicion that the account he had of her was not wholly true, which was that she was a handsome woman but not surpassingly beautiful as had been reputed, not graceful, not charming in manner and conversation. She could save them by justifying his description of her — by using a woman's art to lessen instead of enhancing her natural beauty, by putting away her natural charm and power to fascinate all who approached her.

Thus he pleaded, praying for mercy, even as a captive prays to his conqueror for life, and never once daring to lift his bowed head to look at her face; while she sat motionless and silent, not a word, not a sigh, escaping her; and she was like a woman carved in stone, with knees of stone on which his head rested.

Then, at length, exhausted with his passionate pleading and frightened at her silence and deadly stillness, he raised his head and looked up at her face to behold it radiant and smiling. Then, looking down lovingly into his eyes, she raised her hands to her head, and loosening the great mass of coiled tresses let them fall over him, covering his head and shoulders and back as with a splendid mantle of shining red gold. And he, the awful fear now gone, continued silently gazing up at her, absorbed in her wonderful loveliness.

Bending down she put her arms round his neck and spoke: Do you not know, O Athelwold, that I love you alone and could love no other, noble or king; that without you life would not be life to me? All you have told me endears you more to me, and all you wish me to do shall be done, though it may cause your king and friend to think meanly of you for having given your hand to one so little worthy of you.

She having thus spoken, he was ready to pour forth his gratitude in burning words, but she would not have it. No more words, she said, putting her hand on his mouth. Your anxious day is over — your burden dropped. Rest here on the couch by my side, and let me think on all there is to plan and do against tomorrow evening.

And so they were silent, and he, reclining on the cushions, watched her face and saw her smile and wondered what was passing in her mind to cause that smile. Doubtless it was something to do with the question of her disguising arts.

What had caused her to smile was a happy memory of the days with Athelwold before their marriage, when one day he came in to her with a leather bag in his hand and said: Do you, who are so beautiful yourself, love all beautiful things? And do you love the beauty of gems? And when she replied that she loved gems above all beautiful things, he poured out the contents of his bag in her lap — brilliants, sapphires, rubies, emeralds, opals, pearls in gold setting, in bracelets, necklets, pendants, rings and brooches. And when she gloated over this splendid gift, taking up gem after gem, exclaiming delightedly at its size and colour and lustre, he told her that he once knew a man who maintained that it was a mistake for a beautiful woman to wear gems. Why? she asked, would he have then wholly unadorned? No, he replied, he liked to see them wearing gold, saying that gold makes the most perfect setting for a woman's beauty, just as it does for a precious stone, and its effect is to enhance the beauty it surrounds. But the woman's beauty has its meeting and central point in the eyes, and the light and soul in them illumines the whole face. And in the stone nature simulates the eye, and although without a soul its brilliant light and colour make it the equal of the eye, and therefore when worn as an ornament it competes with the eye, and in effect lessens the beauty it is supposed to enhance. He said that gems should be worn only by women who are not beautiful, who must rely on something extraneous to attract attention, since it would be better to a homely woman that men should look at her to admire a diamond or sapphire than not to look at her at all. She had laughed and asked him who the man was who had such strange ideas, and he had replied that he had forgotten his name.

Now, recalling this incident after so long a time, it all at once flashed into her mind that Edgar was the man he had spoken of; she knew now because, always secretly watchful, she had noted that he never spoke of Edgar or heard Edgar spoken of without a slight subtle change in the expression of his face, also, if he spoke, in the tone of his voice. It was the change that comes into the face, and into the tone, when one remembers or speaks of the person most loved in all the world. And she remembered now that he had that changed expression and tone of voice, when he had spoken of the man whose name he pretended to have forgotten.

And while she sat thinking of this it grew dark in the room, the light of the fire having died down. Then presently, in the profound stillness of the room, she heard the sound of his deep, regular breathing and knew that he slept, and that it was a sweet sleep after his anxious day. Going softly to the hearth she moved the yet still glowing logs, until they sent up a sudden flame and the light fell upon the sleeper's still face. Turning, she gazed steadily at it — the face of the man who had won her; but her own face in the firelight was white and still and wore a strange expression. Now she moved noiselessly to his side and bent down as if to whisper in his ear, but suddenly drew back again and moved towards the door, then turning gazed once more at his face and murmured: No, no, even a word faintly whispered would bring him a dream, and it is better his sleep should be dreamless. For now he has had his day and it is finished, and tomorrow is mine.

VI

On the following day Athelwold was occupied with preparations for the king's reception and for the next day's boar-hunt in the forest. At the same time he was still somewhat anxious as to his wife's more difficult part, and from time to time he came to see and consult with her. He then observed a singular change in her, both in her appearance and conduct. No longer the radiant, loving Elfrida, her beauty now had been dimmed and she was unsmiling and her manner towards him repellant. She had nothing to say to him except that she wished him to leave her alone. Accordingly he withdrew, feeling a little hurt, and at the same time admiring her extraordinary skill in disguising her natural loveliness and charm, but almost fearing that she was making too great a change in her appearance.

Thus passed the day, and in the late afternoon Edgar duly arrived, and when he had rested a little, was conducted to the banqueting-room, where the meeting with Elfrida would take place.

Then Elfrida came, and Athelwold hastened to the entrance to take her hand and conduct her to the king; then, seeing her, he stood still and stared in silent astonishment and dismay at the change he saw in her, for never before had he beheld her so beautiful, so queenly and magnificent. What did it mean — did she wish to destroy him? Seeing the state he was in she placed her hand in his, and murmured softly: I know best. And so, holding her hand, he conducted her to the king, who stood waiting to receive her. For all she had done that day to please and to deceive him had now been undone, and everything that had been possible had been done to enhance her loveliness. She had arrayed herself in a violet-coloured silk gown with a network of gold thread over the body and wide sleeves to the elbows, and rope of gold round her waist with its long ends falling to her knee. The great mass of her coiled hair was surmounted with a golden comb, and golden pendants dropped from her ears to her shoulders. Also she wore gold armlets coiled serpent-wise round her white arms from elbow to wrist. Not a gem — nothing but pale yellow gold.

Edgar himself was amazed at her loveliness, for never had he seen anything comparable to it; and when he gazed into her eyes she did not lower hers, but returned gaze for gaze, and there was that in her eyes and their strange eloquence which kindled a sudden flame of passion in his heart, and for a moment it appeared in his countenance. Then, quickly recovering himself, he greeted her graciously but with his usual kingly dignity of manner, and for the rest of the time he conversed with her and Athelwold in such a pleasant and friendly way that his host began to recover somewhat from his apprehensions. But in his heart Edgar was saying: And this is the woman that Athelwold, the close friend of all my days, from boyhood until now, the one man in the world I loved and trusted, has robbed me of!

And Athelwold at the same time was revolving in his mind the mystery of Elfrida's action. What did she mean when she whispered to him that she knew best? And why, when she wished to appear in that magnificent way before the king, had she worn nothing but gold ornaments — not one of the splendid gems of which she possessed such a store?

She had remembered something which he had forgotten.

Now when the two friends were left alone together drinking wine, Athelwold was still troubled in his mind, although his suspicion and fear were not so acute as at first, and the longer they sat talking — until the small hours — the more relieved did he feel from Edgar's manner towards him. Edgar in his cups opened his heart and was more loving and free in his speech than ever before. He loved Athelwold as he loved no one else in the world, and to see him great and happy was his first desire; and he congratulated him from his heart on having found a wife who was worthy of him and would eventually bring him, through her father, such great possessions as would make him the chief nobleman in the land. All happiness and glory to them both; and when a child was born to them he would be its godfather, and if happily by that time there was a queen, she should be its godmother.

Then he recalled their happy boyhood's days in East Anglia, that joyful time when they first hunted and had many a mishap and fell from their horses when they pursued hare and deer and bustard in the wide open stretches of sandy country; and in the autumn and winter months when they were wild-fowling in the great level flooded lands where the geese and all wild-fowl came in clouds and myriads. And now he laughed and now his eyes grew moist at the recollection of the irrecoverable glad days.

Little time was left for sleep; yet they were ready early next morning for the day's great boar-hunt in the forest, and only when the king was about to mount his horse did Elfrida make her appearance. She came out to him from the door, not richly dressed now, but in a simple white linen robe and not an ornament on her except that splendid crown of the red-gold hair on her head. And her face too was almost colourless now, and grave and still. She brought wine in a golden cup and gave it to the king, and he once more fixed his eyes on her and for some moments they continued silently gazing, each in that fixed gaze seeming to devour the secrets of the other's soul. Then she wished him a happy hunting, and he said in reply he hoped it would be the happiest hunting he had ever had. Then, after drinking the wine, he mounted his horse and rode away. And she remained standing very still, the cup in her hand, gazing after him as he rode side by side with Athelwold, until in the distance the trees hid him from her sight.

Now when they had ridden a distance of three miles or more into the heart of the forest, they came to a broad drive-like stretch of green turf, and the king cried: This is just what I have been wishing for! Come, let us give our horses a good gallop. And when they loosened the reins, the horses, glad to have a race on such a ground, instantly sprang forward; but Edgar, keeping a tight rein, was presently left twenty or thirty yards behind; then, setting spurs to his horse, he dashed forward, and on coming abreast of his companion, drew his knife and struck him in the back, dealing the blow with such a concentrated fury that the knife was buried almost to the hilt. Then violently wrenching it out, he would have struck again had not the earl, with a scream of agony, tumbled from his seat. The horse, freed from its rider, rushed on in a sudden panic, and the king's horse side by side with it. Edgar, throwing himself back and exerting his whole strength, succeeded in bringing him to a stop at a distance of fifty or sixty yards, then turning, came riding back at a furious speed.

Now when Athelwold fell, all those who were riding behind, the earl's and the king's men to the number of thirty or forty, dashed forward, and some of them, hurriedly dismounting, gathered about him as he lay groaning and writhing and pouring out his blood on the ground. But at the king's approach they drew quickly back to make way for him, and he came straight on and caused his horse to trample on the fallen man. Then pointing to him with the knife he still had in his hand, he cried: That is how I serve a false friend and traitor! Then, wiping the stained knife-blade on his horse's neck and sheathing it, he shouted: Back to Salisbury! and setting spurs to his horse, galloped off towards the Andover road.

His men immediately mounted and followed, leaving the earl's men with their master. Lifting him up, they placed him on a horse, and with a mounted man on each side to hold him up, they moved back at a walking pace towards Wherwell.

Messengers were sent ahead to inform Elfrida of what had happened, and then, an hour later, yet another messenger to tell that Athelwold, when half-way home, had breathed his last. Then at last the corpse was brought to the castle and she met it with tears and lamentations. But afterwards in her own chamber, when she had dismissed all her attendants, as she desired to weep alone, her grief changed to joy. O, glorious Edgar, she said, the time will come when you will know what I feel now, when at your feet, embracing your knees and kissing the blessed hand that with one blow has given me life and liberty. One blow and your revenge was satisfied and you had won me; I know it, I saw it all in that flame of love and fury in your eyes at our first meeting, which you permitted me to see, which, if he had seen, he would have known that he was doomed. O perfect master of dissimulation, all the more do I love and worship you for dealing with him as he dealt with you and with me; caressing him with flattering words until the moment came to strike and slay. And I love you all the more for making your horse trample on him as he lay bleeding his life out on the ground. And now you have opened the way with your knife you shall come back or call me to you when it pleases you, and for the rest of your life it will be a satisfaction to you to know that you have taken a modest woman as well as the fairest in the land for wife and queen, and your pride in me will be my happiness and glory. For men's love is little to me since Athelwold taught me to think meanly of all men, except you that slew him. And you shall be free to follow your own mind and be ever strenuous and vigilant and run after kingly pleasures, pursuing deer and wolf and beautiful women all over the land. And I shall listen to the tales of your adventures and conquests with a smile like that of a mother who sees her child playing seriously with its dolls and toys, talking to and caressing them. And in return you shall give me my desire, which is power and splendour; for these I crave, to be first and greatest, to raise up and cast down, and in all our life I shall be your help and stay in ruling this realm, so that our names may be linked together and shine in the annals of England for all time.

When Edgar slew Athelwold his age was twenty-two, and before he was a year older he had married Elfrida, to the rage of that great man and primate and more than premier, who, under Edgar, virtually ruled England. And in his rage, and remembering how he had dealt with a previous boy king, whose beautiful young wife he had hounded to her dreadful end, he charged Elfrida with having instigated her husband's murder, and commanded the king to put that woman away. This roused the man and passionate lover, and the tiger in the man, in Edgar, and the wise and subtle-minded ecclesiastic quickly recognised that he had set himself against one of a will more powerful and dangerous than his own. He remembered that it was Edgar, who, when he had been deprived of his abbey and driven in disgrace from the land, had recalled and made him so great, and he knew that the result of a quarrel between them would be a mighty upheaval in the land and the sweeping away of all his great reforms. And so, cursing the woman in his heart and secretly vowing vengeance on her, he was compelled in the interests of the Church to acquiesce in this fresh crime of the king.

VII

Eight years had passed since the king's marriage with Elfrida, and the one child born to them was now seven, the darling of his parents, Ethelred the angelic child, who to the end of his long life would be praised for one thing only — his personal beauty. But Edward, his half-brother, now in his thirteenth year, was regarded by her with an almost equal affection, on account of his beauty and charm, his devotion to his step-mother, the only mother he had known, and, above all, for his love of his little half-brother. He was never happy unless he was with him, acting the part of guide and instructor as well as playfellow.

Edgar had recently completed one of his great works, the building of Corfe Castle, and now whenever he was in Wessex preferred it as a residence, since he loved best that part of England with its wide moors and hunting forests, and its neighbourhood to the sea and to Portland and Poole water. He had been absent for many weeks on a journey to Northumbria, and the last tidings of his movements were that he was on his way to the south, travelling on the Welsh border, and intended visiting the Abbot of Glastonbury before returning to Dorset. This religious house was already very great in his day; he had conferred many benefits on it, and contemplated still others.

It was summer time, a season of great heats, and Elfrida with the two little princes often went to the coast to spend a whole day in the open air by the sea. Her favourite spot was at the foot of a vast chalk down with a slight strip of woodland between its lowest slope and the beach. She was at this spot one day about noon where the trees were few and large, growing wide apart, and had settled herself on a pile of cushions placed at the roots of a big old oak tree, where from her seat she could look out over the blue expanse of water. But the hamlet and church close by on her left hand were hidden by the wood, though sounds issuing from it could be heard occasionally — shouts and bursts of laughter, and at times the music of a stringed instrument and a voice singing. These sounds came from her armed guard and other attendants who were speeding the idle hours of waiting in their own way, in eating and drinking and in games and dancing. Only two women remained to attend to her wants, and one armed man to keep watch and guard over the two boys at their play.

They were not now far off, not above fifty yards, among the big trees; but for hours past they had been away out of her sight, racing on their ponies over the great down; then bathing in the sea, Edward teaching his little brother to swim; then he had given him lessons in tree-climbing, and now, tired of all these exertions, and for variety's sake, they were amusing themselves by standing on their heads. Little Ethelred had tried and failed repeatedly, then at last, with hands and head firmly planted on the sward, he had succeeded in throwing his legs up and keeping them in a vertical position for a few seconds, this feat being loudly applauded by his young instructor.

Elfrida, who had witnessed this display from her seat, burst out laughing, then said to herself: O how I love these two beautiful boys almost with an equal love, albeit one is not mine! But Edward must be ever dear to me because of his sweetness and his love of me and, even more, his love and tender care of my darling. Yet am I not wholly free from an anxious thought of the distant future. Ah, no, let me not think of such a thing! This sweet child of a boy-father and girl-mother — the frail mother that died in her teens — he can never grow to be a proud, masterful, ambitious man — never aspire to wear his father's crown! Edgar's first-born, it is true, but not mine, and he can never be king. For Edgar and I are one; is it conceivable that he should oppose me in this — that we that are one in mind and soul shall at the last be divided and at enmity? Have we not said it an hundred times that we are one? One in all things except in passion. Yet this very coldness in me in which I differ from others is my chief strength and glory, and has made our two lives one life. And when he is tired and satiated with the common beauty and the common passions of other women he returns to me only to have his first love kindled afresh, and when in love and pity I give myself to him and am his bride afresh as when first he had my body in his arms, it is to him as if one of the immortals had stooped to a mortal, and he tells me I am the flower of womankind and of the world, that my white body is a perfect white flower, my hair a shining gold flower, my mouth a fragrant scarlet flower, and my eyes a sacred blue flower, surpassing all others in loveliness. And when I have satisfied him, and the tempest in his blood has abated, then for the rapture he has had I have mine, when, ashamed at his violence, as if it had been an insult to me, he covers his face with my hair and sheds tears of love and contrition on my breasts. O nothing can ever disunite us! Even from the first, before I ever saw him, when he was coming to me I knew that we were destined to be one. And he too knew it from the moment of seeing me, and knew that I knew it; and when he sat at meat with us and looked smilingly at the friend of his bosom and spoke merrily to him, and resolved at the same time to take his life, he knew that by so doing he would fulfil my desire, and as my knowledge of the betrayal was first, so the desire to shed that abhorred blood was in me first. Nevertheless, I cannot be free of all anxious thoughts, and fear too of my implacable enemy and traducer who from a distance watches all my movements, who reads Edgar's mind even as he would a book, and what he finds there writ by me he seeks to blot out; and thus does he ever thwart me. But though I cannot measure my strength against his, it will not always be so, seeing that he is old and I am young, with Time and Death on my side, who will like good and faithful servants bring him to the dust, so that my triumph must come. And when he is no more I shall have time to unbuild the structure he has raised with lies for stones and my name coupled with some evil deed cut in every stone. For I look ever to the future, even to the end to see this Edgar, with the light of life shining so brightly in him now, a venerable king with silver hair, his passions cool, his strength failing, leaning more heavily on me; until at last, persuaded by me, he will step down from the throne and resign his crown to our son — our Ethelred. And in him and his son after him, and in his son's sons we shall live still in their blood, and with them rule this kingdom of Edgar the Peaceful — a realm of everlasting peace.

Thus she mused, until overcome by her swift, crowding thoughts and passions, love and hate, with memories dreadful or beautiful, of her past and strivings of her mind to pierce the future, she burst into a violent storm of tears so that her frame was shaken, and covering her eyes with her hands she strove to get the better of her agitation lest her weakness should be witnessed by her attendants. But when this tempest had left her and she lifted her eyes again, it seemed to her that the burning tears which had relieved her heart had also washed away some trouble that had been like a dimness on all visible nature, and earth and sea and sky were glorified as if the sunlight flooding the world fell direct from the heavenly throne, and she sat drinking in pure delight from the sight of it and the soft, warm air she breathed.

Then, to complete her happiness, the silence that reigned around her was broken by a sweet, musical sound of a little bird that sang from the tree-top high above her head. This was the redstart, and the tree under which she sat was its singing-tree, to which it resorted many times a day to spend half an hour or so repeating its brief song at intervals of a few seconds — a small song that was like the song of the redbreast, subdued, refined and spiritualised, as of a spirit that lived within the tree.

Listening to it in that happy, tender mood which had followed her tears, she gazed up and tried to catch sight of it, but could see nothing but the deep-cut, green, translucent, clustering oak leaves showing the blue of heaven and shining like emeralds in the sunlight. O sweet, blessed little bird, she said, are you indeed a bird? I think you are a messenger sent to assure me that all my hopes and dreams of the distant days to come will be fulfilled. Sing again and again and again; I could listen for hours to that selfsame song.

But she heard it no more; the bird had flown away. Then, still listening, she caught a different sound — the loud hoof-beats of horses being ridden at furious speed towards the hamlet. Listening intently to that sound she heard, on its arrival at the hamlet, a sudden, great cry as if all the men gathered there had united their voices in one cry; and she stood up, and her women came to her, and all together stood silently gazing in that direction. Then the two boys who had been lying on the turf not far off came running to them and caught her by the hands, one on each side, and Edward, looking up at her white, still face, cried, Mother, what is it you fear? But she answered no word. Then again the sound of hoofs was heard and they knew the riders were now coming at a swift gallop to them. And in a few moments they appeared among the trees, and reining up their horses at a distance of some yards, one sprang to the ground, and advancing to the queen, made his obeisance, then told her he had been sent to inform her of Edgar's death. He had been seized by a sudden violent fever in Gloucestershire, on his way to Glastonbury, and had died after two days' illness. He had been unconscious all the time, but more than once he had cried out, On to Glastonbury! and now in obedience to that command his body was being conveyed thither for interment at the abbey.

VIII

She had no tears to shed, no word to say, nor was there any sense of grief at her loss. She had loved him — once upon a time; she had always admired him for his better qualities; even his excessive pride and ostentation had been pleasing to her; finally she had been more than tolerant of his vices or weaknesses, regarding them as matters beneath her attention. Nevertheless, in their eight years of married life they had become increasingly repugnant to her stronger and colder nature. He had degenerated, bodily and mentally, and was not now like that shining one who had come to her at Wherwell Castle, who had not hesitated to strike the blow that had set her free. The tidings of his death had all at once sprung the truth on her mind that the old love was dead, that it had indeed been long dead, and that she had actually come to despise him.

But what should she do — what be — without him! She had been his queen, loved to adoration, and he had been her shield; now she was alone, face to face with her bitter, powerful enemy. Now it seemed to her that she had been living in a beautiful peaceful land, a paradise of fruit and flowers and all delightful things; that in a moment, as by a miracle, it had turned to a waste of black ashes still hot and smoking from the desolating flames that had passed over it. But she was not one to give herself over to despondency so long as there was anything to be done. Very quickly she roused herself to action, and despatched messengers to all those powerful friends who shared her hatred of the great archbishop, and would be glad of the opportunity now offered of wresting the rule from his hands. Until now he had triumphed because he had had the king to support him even in his most arbitrary and tyrannical measures; now was the time to show a bold front, to proclaim her son as the right successor, and with herself, assisted by chosen councillors to direct her boy, the power would be in her hands, and once more, as in King Edwin's day, the great Dunstan, disgraced and denounced, would be compelled to fly from the country lest a more dreadful punishment should befall him. Finally, leaving the two little princes at Corfe Castle, she travelled to Mercia to be with and animate her powerful friends and fellow-plotters with her presence.

All their plottings and movements were known to Dunstan, and he was too quick for them. Whilst they, divided among themselves, were debating and arranging their plans, he had called together all the leading bishops and councillors of the late king, and they had agreed that Edward must be proclaimed as the first-born; and although but a boy of thirteen, the danger to the country would not be so great as it would to give the succession to a child of seven years. Accordingly Edward was proclaimed king and removed from Corfe Castle while the queen was still absent in Mercia.

For a while it looked as if this bold and prompt act on the part of Dunstan would have led to civil war; but a great majority of the nobles gave their adhesion to Edward, and Elfrida's friends soon concluded that they were not strong enough to set her boy up and try to overthrow Edward, or to divide England again between two boy kings as in Edwin and Edgar's early years.

She accordingly returned discomfited to Corfe and to her child, now always crying for his beloved brother who had been taken from him; and there was not in all England a more miserable woman than Elfrida the queen. For after this defeat she could hope no more; her power was gone past recovery — all that had made her life beautiful and glorious was gone. Now Corfe was like that other castle at Wherwell, where Earl Athelwold had kept her like a caged bird for his pleasure when he visited her; only worse, since she was eight years younger then, her beauty fresher, her heart burning with secret hopes and ambitions, and the great world where there were towns and a king, and many noble men and women gathered round him yet to be known. And all these things had come to her and were now lost — now nothing was left but bitterest regrets and hatred of all those who had failed her at the last. Hatred first of all and above all of her great triumphant enemy, and hatred of the boy king she had loved with a mother's love until now, and cherished for many years. Hatred too of herself when she recalled the part she had recently played in Mercia, where she had not disdained to practise all her fascinating arts on many persons she despised in order to bind them to her cause, and had thereby given cause to her monkish enemy to charge her with immodesty. It was with something like hatred too that she regarded her own child when he would come crying to her, begging her to take him to his beloved brother; carried away with sudden rage, she would strike and thrust him violently from her, then order her women to take him away and keep him out of her sight.

Three years had gone by, during which she had continued living alone at Corfe, still under a cloud and nursing her bitter revengeful feeling in her heart, until that fatal afternoon on the eighteenth day of March, 978.

The young king, now in his seventeenth year, had come to these favourite hunting-grounds of his late father, and was out hunting on that day. He had lost sight of his companions in a wood or thicket of thorn and furze, and galloping in search of them he came out from the wood on the further side; and there before him, not a mile away, was Corfe Castle, his old beloved home, and the home still of the two beings he loved best in the world — his step-mother and his little half-brother. And although he had been sternly warned that they were his secret enemies, that it would be dangerous to hold any intercourse with them, the sight of the castle and his craving to look again on their dear faces overcame his scruples. There would be no harm, no danger to him and no great disobedience on his part to ride to the gates and see and greet them without dismounting.

When Elfrida was told that Edward himself was at the gates calling to her and Ethelred to come out to him she became violently excited, and cried out that God himself was on her side, and had delivered the boy into her hands. She ordered her servants to go out and persuade him to come in to her, to take away his horse as soon as he had dismounted, and not to allow him to leave the castle. Then, when they returned to say the king refused to dismount and again begged them to go to him, she went to the gates, but without the boy, and greeted him joyfully, while he, glad at the meeting, bent down and embraced her and kissed her face. But when she refused to send for Ethelred, and urged him persistently to dismount and come in to see his little brother who was crying for him, he began to notice the extreme excitement which burned in her eyes and made her voice tremble, and beginning to fear some design against him, he refused again more firmly to obey her wish; then she, to gain time, sent for wine for him to drink before parting from her. And during all this time while his departure was being delayed, her people, men and women, had been coming out until, sitting on his horse, he was in the midst of a crowd, and these too all looked on him with excited faces, which increased his apprehension, so that when he had drunk the wine he all at once set spurs to his horse to break away from among them. Then she, looking at her men, cried out: Is this the way you serve me? And no sooner had the words fallen from her lips than one man bounded forward, like a hound on its quarry, and coming abreast of the horse, dealt the king a blow with his knife in the side. The next moment the horse and rider were free of the crowd and rushing away over the moor. A cry of horror had burst from the women gathered there when the blow was struck; now all were silent, watching with white, scared faces as he rode swiftly away. Then presently they saw him swerve on his horse, then fall, with his right foot still remaining caught in the stirrup, and that the panic-stricken horse was dragging him at furious speed over the rough moor.

Only then the queen spoke, and in an agitated voice told them to mount and follow; and charged them that if they overtook the horse and found that the king had been killed, to bury the body where it would not be found, so that the manner of his death should not be known.

When the men returned they reported that they had found the dead body of the king a mile away, where the horse had got free of it, and they had buried it in a thicket where it would never be discovered.

IX

When Edward in sudden terror set spurs to his horse: when at the same moment a knife flashed out and the fatal blow was delivered, Elfrida too, like the other women witnesses in the crowd, had uttered a cry of horror. But once the deed was accomplished and the assurance received that the body had been hidden where it would never be found, the feeling experienced at the spectacle was changed to one of exultation. For now at last, after three miserable years of brooding on her defeat, she had unexpectedly triumphed, and it was as if she already had her foot set on her enemies' necks. For now her boy would be king — happily there was no other candidate in the field; now her great friends from all over the land would fly to her aid, and with them for her councillors she would practically be the ruler during the king's long minority.

Thus she exulted; then, when that first tempest of passionate excitement had abated, came a revulsion of feeling when the vivid recollections of that pitiful scene returned and would not be thrust away; when she saw again the change from affection and delight at beholding her to suspicion and fear, then terror, come into the face of the boy she had loved; when she witnessed the dreadful blow and watched him when he swerved and fell from the saddle and the frightened horse galloped wildly away dragging him over the rough moor. For now she knew that in her heart she had never hated him: the animosity had been only on the surface and was an overflow of her consuming hatred of the primate. She had always loved the boy, and now that he no longer stood in her way to power she loved him again. And she had slain him! O no, she was thankful to think she had not! His death had come about by chance. Her commands to her people had been that he was not to be allowed to leave the castle; she had resolved to detain him, to hide and hold him a captive, to persuade or in some way compel him to abdicate in his brother's favour. She could not now say just how she had intended to deal with him, but it was never her intention to murder him. Her commands had been misunderstood, and she could not be blamed for his death, however much she was to benefit by it. God would not hold her accountable.

Could she then believe that she was guiltless in God's sight? Alas! on second thoughts she dared not affirm it. She was guiltless only in the way that she had been guiltless of Athelwold's murder; had she not rejoiced at the part she had had in that act? Athelwold had deserved his fate, and she had never repented that deed, nor had Edgar. She had not dealt the fatal blow then nor now, but she had wished for Edward's death even as she had wished for Athelwold's, and it was for her the blow was struck. It was a difficult and dreadful question. She was not equal to it. Let it be put off, the pressing question now was, what would man's judgment be — how would she now stand before the world?

And now the hope came that the secret of the king's disappearance would never be known; that after a time it would be assumed that he was dead, and that his death would never be traced to her door.

A vain hope, as she quickly found! There had been too many witnesses of the deed both of the castle people and those who lived outside the gates. The news spread fast and far as if carried by winged messengers, so that it was soon known throughout the kingdom, and everywhere it was told and believed that the queen herself had dealt the fatal blow.

Not Elfrida nor any one living at that time could have foretold the effect on the people generally of this deed, described as the foulest which had been done in Saxon times. There had in fact been a thousand blacker deeds in the England of that dreadful period, but never one that touched the heart and imagination of the whole people in the same way. Furthermore, it came after a long pause, a serene interval of many years in the everlasting turmoil — the years of the reign of Edgar the Peaceful, whose early death had up till then been its one great sorrow. A time too of recovery from a state of insensibility to evil deeds; of increasing civilisation and the softening of hearts. For Edward was the child of Edgar and his child-wife, who was beautiful and beloved and died young; and he had inherited the beauty, charm, and all engaging qualities of his parents. It is true that these qualities were known at first-hand only by those who were about him; but from these the feeling inspired had been communicated to those outside in ever-widening circles until it was spread over all the land, so that there was no habitation, from the castle to the hovel, in which the name of Edward was not as music on man's lips. And we of the present generation can perhaps understand this better than those of any other in the past centuries, for having a prince and heir to the English throne of this same name so great in our annals, one as universally loved as was Edward the Second, afterwards called the Martyr, in his day.

One result of this general outburst of feeling was that all those who had been, openly or secretly, in alliance with Elfrida now hastened to dissociate themselves from her. She was told that by her own rash act in killing the king before the world she had ruined her own cause for ever.

And Dunstan was not defeated after all. He made haste to proclaim the son, the boy of ten years, king of England, and at the same time to denounce the mother as a murderess. Nor did she dare to resist him when he removed the little prince from Corfe Castle and placed him with some of his own creatures, with monks for schoolmasters and guardians, whose first lesson to him would be detestation of his mother. This lesson too had to be impressed on the public mind; and at once, in obedience to this command, every preaching monk in every chapel in the land raged against the queen, the enemy of the archbishop and of religion, the tigress in human shape, and author of the greatest crime known in the land since Cerdic's landing. No fortitude could stand against such a storm of execration. It overwhelmed her. It was, she believed, a preparation for the dreadful doom about to fall on her. This was her great enemy's day, and he would no longer be baulked of his revenge. She remembered that Edwin had died by the assassin's hand, and the awful fate of his queen Elgitha, whose too beautiful face was branded with hot irons, and who was hamstrung and left to perish in unimaginable agony. She was like the hunted roe deer hiding in a close thicket and listening, trembling, to the hunters shouting and blowing on their horns and to the baying of their dogs, seeking for her in the wood.

Could she defend herself against them in her castle? She consulted her guard as to this, with the result that most of the men secretly left her. There was nothing for her to do but wait in dreadful suspense, and thereafter she would spend many hours every day in a tower commanding a wide view of the surrounding level country to watch the road with anxious eyes. But the feared hunters came not; the sound of the cry for vengeance grew fainter and fainter until it died into silence. It was at length borne in on her that she was not to be punished — at all events, not here and by man. It came as a surprise to every one, herself included. But it had been remembered that she was Edgar's widow and the king's mother, and that her power and influence were dead. Never again would she lift her head in England. Furthermore, Dunstan was growing old; and albeit his zeal for religion, pure and undefiled as he understood it, was not abated, the cruel, ruthless instincts and temper, which had accompanied and made it effective in the great day of conflict when he was engaged in sweeping from England the sin and scandal of a married clergy, had by now burnt themselves out. Vengeance is mine, saith the Lord, I will repay, and he was satisfied to have no more to do with her. Let the abhorred woman answer to God for her crimes.

But now that all fear of punishment by man was over, this dreadful thought that she was answerable to God weighed more and more heavily on her. Nor could she escape by day or night from the persistent image of the murdered boy. It haunted her like a ghost in every room, and when she climbed to a tower to look out it was to see his horse rushing madly away dragging his bleeding body over the moor. Or when she went out to the gate it was still to find him there, sitting on his horse, his face lighting up with love and joy at beholding her again; then the change — the surprise, the fear, the wine-cup, the attempt to break away, her cry — the unconsidered words she had uttered — and the fatal blow! The cry that rose from all England calling on God to destroy her! would that be her torment — would it sound in her ears through all eternity?

Corfe became unendurable to her, and eventually she moved to Bere, in Dorset, where the lands were her property and she possessed a house of her own, and there for upwards of a year she resided in the strictest seclusion.

It then came out and was quickly noised abroad that the king's body had been discovered long ago — miraculously it was said — in that brake near Corfe where it had been hidden; that it had been removed to and secretly buried at Wareham, and it was also said that miracles were occurring at that spot. This caused a fresh outburst of excitement in the country; the cry of miracles roused the religious houses all over Wessex, and there was a clamour for possession of the remains. This was a question for the heads of the Church to decide, and it was eventually decreed that the monastery of Shaftesbury, founded by King Alfred,

Edward's great-great-grandfather, should have the body. Shaftesbury then, in order to advertise so important an acquisition to the world, resolved to make the removal of the remains the occasion of a great ceremony, a magnificent procession bearing the sacred remains from Wareham to the distant little city on the hill, attended by representatives from religious houses all over the country and by the pious generally.

Elfrida, sitting alone in her house, brooding on her desolation, heard of all these happenings and doings with increasing excitement; then all at once resolved to take part herself in the procession. This was seemingly a strange, almost incredible departure for one of her indomitable character and so embittered against the primate, even as he was against her. But her fight with him was now ended; she was defeated, broken, deprived of everything that she valued in life; it was time to think about the life to come. Furthermore, it now came to her that this was not her own thought, but that it had been whispered to her soul by some compassionate being of a higher order, and it was suggested to her that here was an opportunity for a first step towards a reconciliation with God and man. She dared not disregard it. Once more she would appear before the world, not as the beautiful, magnificent Elfrida, the proud and powerful woman of other days, but as a humble penitent doing her bitter penance in public, one of a thousand or ten thousand humble pilgrims, clad in mean garments, riding only when overcome with fatigue, and at the last stage of that long twenty-five-mile journey casting off her shoes to climb the steep stony road on naked, bleeding feet.

This resolution, in which she was strongly supported by the local priesthood, had a mollifying effect on the people, and something like compassion began to mingle with their feelings of hatred towards her. But when it was reported to Dunstan, he fell into a rage, and imagined or pretended to believe that some sinister design was hidden under it. She was the same woman, he said, who had instigated the murder of her first husband by means of a trick of this kind. She must not be allowed to show her face again. He then despatched a stern and threatening message forbidding her to take any part in or show herself at the procession.

This came at the last moment when all her preparations had been made; but she dared not disobey. The effect was to increase her misery. It was as if the gates of mercy and deliverance, which had been opened, miraculously as she believed, had now been once more closed against her; and it was also as if her enemy had said: I have spared you the branding with hot irons and slashing of sinews with sharp knives, not out of compassion, but in order to subject you to a more terrible punishment.

Despair possessed her, which turned to sullen rage when she found that the feeling of the people around her had again become hostile, owing to the report that her non-appearance at the procession was due to the discovery by Dunstan in good time of a secret plot against the State on her part. Her house at Bere became unendurable to her; she resolved to quit it, and made choice of Salisbury as her next place of residence. It was not far to go, and she had a good house there which had not been used since Edgar's death, but was always kept ready for her occupation.

X

It was about the middle of the afternoon when Elfrida on horseback and attended by her mounted guard of twenty or more men, followed by a convoy of carts with her servants and luggage, arrived at Salisbury, and was surprised and disturbed at the sight of a vast concourse of people standing without the gates.

It had got abroad that she was coming to Salisbury on that day, and it was also now known throughout Wessex that she had not been allowed to attend the procession to Shaftesbury. This had excited the people, and a large part of the inhabitants of the town and the adjacent hamlets had congregated to witness her arrival.

On her approach the crowd opened out on either side to make way for her and her men, and glancing to this side and that she saw that every pair of eyes in all that vast silent crowd were fixed intently on her face.

Then came a fresh surprise when she found a mounted guard standing with drawn swords before the gates. The captain of the guard, lifting his hand, cried out to her to halt, then in a loud voice he informed her he had been ordered to turn her back from the gates. Was it then to witness this fresh insult that the people had now been brought together? Anger and apprehension struggled for mastery in her breast and choked her utterance when she attempted to speak. She could only turn to her men, and in instant response to her look they drew their swords and pressed forward as if about to force their way in. This movement on their part was greeted with a loud burst of derisive laughter from the town guard. Then from out of the middle of the crowd of lookers-on came a cry of Murderess! quickly followed by another shout of Go back, murderess, you are not wanted here! This was a signal for all the unruly spirits in the throng — all those whose delight is to trample upon the fallen — and from all sides there arose a storm of jeers and execrations, and it was as if she was in the midst of a frantic bellowing herd eager to gore and trample her to death. And these were the same people that a few short years ago would rush out from their houses to gaze with pride and delight at her, their beautiful queen, and applaud her to the echo whenever she appeared at their gates! Now, better than ever before, she realised the change of feeling towards her from affectionate loyalty to abhorrence, and drained to the last bitterest dregs the cup of shame and humiliation.

With trembling hand she turned her horse round, and bending her ashen white face low rode slowly out of the crowd, her men close to her on either side, threatening with their swords those that pressed nearest and followed in their retreat by shouts and jeers. But when well out of sight and sound of the people she dismounted and sat down on the turf to rest and consider what was to be done. By and by a mounted man was seen coming from Salisbury at a fast gallop. He came with a letter and message to the queen from an aged nobleman, one she had known in former years at court. He informed her that he owned a large house at or near Amesbury which he could not now use on account of his age and infirmities, which compelled him to remain in Salisbury. This house she might occupy for as long as she wished to remain in the neighbourhood. He had received permission from the governor of the town to offer it to her, and the only condition was that she must not return to Salisbury.

There was thus one friend left to the reviled and outcast queen — this aged dying man!

Once more she set forth with the messenger as guide, and about set of sun arrived at the house, which was to be her home for the next two to three years, in this darkest period of her life. Yet she could not have found a habitation and surroundings more perfectly suited to her wants and the mood she was in. The house, which was large enough to accommodate all her people, was on the west side of the Avon, a quarter of a mile below Amesbury and two to three hundred yards distant from the river bank, and was surrounded by enclosed land with gardens and orchards, the river itself forming the boundary on one side. Here was the perfect seclusion she desired: here she could spend her hours and days as she ever loved to do in the open air without sight of any human countenance excepting those of her own people, since now strange faces had become hateful to her. Then, again, she loved riding, and just outside of her gates was the great green expanse of the Downs, where she could spend hours on horseback without meeting or seeing a human figure except occasionally a solitary shepherd guarding his flock. So great was the attraction the Downs had for her she herself marvelled at it. It was not merely the sense of power and freedom the rider feels on a horse with the exhilarating effect of swift motion and a wide horizon. Here she had got out of the old and into a new world better suited to her changed spirit. For in that world of men and women in which she had lived until now all nature had become interfused with her own and other people's lives — passions and hopes and fears and dreams and ambitions. Now it was as if an obscuring purple mist had been blown away, leaving the prospect sharp and clear to her sight as it had never appeared before. A wide prospect, whose grateful silence was only broken by the cry or song of some wild bird. Great thickets of dwarf thorn tree and brambles and gorse, aflame with yellow flowers or dark to blackness by contrast with the pale verdure of the earth. And open reaches of elastic turf, its green suffused or sprinkled with red or blue or yellow, according to the kind of flowers proper to the season and place. The sight, too, of wild creatures: fallow deer, looking yellow in the distance when seen amid the black gorse; a flock of bustards taking to flight on her approach would rush away, their spread wings flashing silver-white in the brilliant sunshine. She was like them on her horse, borne swiftly as on wings above the earth, but always near it. Then, casting her eyes up, she would watch the soarers, the buzzards, or harriers and others, circling up from earth on broad motionless wings, bird above bird, ever rising and diminishing to fade away at last into the universal blue. Then, as if aspiring too, she would seek the highest point on some high down, and sitting on her horse survey the prospect before her — the sea of rounded hills, hills beyond hills, stretching away to the dim horizon, and over it all the vast blue dome of heaven. Sky and earth, with thorny brakes and grass and flowers and wild creatures, with birds that flew low and others soaring up into heaven — what was the secret meaning it had for her? She was like one groping for a key in a dark place. Not a human figure visible, not a sign of human occupancy on that expanse! Was this then the secret of her elation? The all-powerful, dreadful God she was at enmity with, whom she feared and fled from, was not here. He, or his spirit, was where man inhabited, in cities and other centres of population, where there were churches and monasteries.

To think this was a veritable relief to her. God was where men worshipped him, and not here! She hugged the new belief and it made her bold and defiant. Doubtless, if he is here, she would say, and can read my thoughts, my horse in his very next gallop will put his foot in a mole-run, and bring me down and break my neck. Or when yon black cloud comes over me, if it is a thunder-cloud, the lightning out of it will strike me dead. If he will but listen to his servant Dunstan this will surely happen. Was it God or the head shepherd of his sheep, here in England, who, when I tried to enter the fold, beat me off with his staff and set his dogs on me so that I was driven away, torn and bleeding, to hide myself in a solitary place? Would it then be better for me to go with my cries for mercy to his seat? O no, I could not come to him there; his doorkeepers would bar the way, and perhaps bring together a crowd of their people to howl at me — Go away, Murderess, you are not wanted here!

Now in spite of those moments, or even hours, of elation, during which her mind would recover its old independence until the sense of freedom was like an intoxication; when she cried out against God that he was cruel and unjust in his dealings with his creatures, that he had raised up and given power to the man who held the rod over her, one who in God's holy name had committed crimes infinitely greater than hers, and she refused to submit to him — in spite of it all she could never shake off the terrible thought that in the end, at God's judgment seat, she would have to answer for her own dark deeds. She could not be free of her religion. She was like one who tears a written paper to pieces and scatters the pieces in anger to see them blown away like snow-flakes on the wind; who by and by discovers one small fragment clinging to his garments, and looking at the half a dozen words and half words appearing on it, adds others from memory or of his own invention. So she with what was left when she thrust her religion away built for herself a different one which was yet like the old; and even here in this solitude she was able to find a house and sacred place for meditation and prayer, in which she prayed indirectly to the God she was at enmity with. For now invariably on returning from her ride to her house at Amesbury she would pay a visit to the Great Stones, the ancient temple of Stonehenge. Dismounting, she would order her attendants to take her horse away and wait for her at a distance, so as not to be disturbed by the sound of their talking. Going in she would seat herself on the central or altar stone and give a little time to meditation — to the tuning of her mind. That circle of rough-hewn stones, rough with grey lichen, were the pillars of her cathedral, with the infinite blue sky for roof, and for incense the smell of flowers and aromatic herbs, and for music the far-off faintly heard sounds that came to her from the surrounding wilderness — the tremulous bleating of sheep and the sudden wild cry of hawk or stone curlew. Closing her eyes she would summon the familiar image and vision of the murdered boy, always coming so quickly, so vividly, that she had brought herself to believe that it was not a mere creation of her own mind and of remorse, a memory, but that he was actually there with her. Moving her hand over the rough stone she would by and by let it rest, pressing it on the stone, and would say, Now I have your hand in mine, and am looking with my soul's eyes into yours, listen again to the words I have spoken so many times. You would not be here if you did not remember me and pity and even love me still. Know then that I am now alone in the world, that I am hated by the world because of your bitter death. And there is not now one living being in the world that I love, for I have ceased to love even my own boy, your old beloved playmate, seeing that he has long been taken from me and taught with all others to despise and hate me. And of all those who inhabit the regions above, in all that innumerable multitude of angels and saints, and of all who have died on earth and been forgiven, you alone have any feeling of compassion for me and can intercede for me. Plead for me — plead for me, O my son; for who is there in heaven or earth that can plead so powerfully for me that am stained with your blood!

Then, having finished her prayer, and wiped away all trace of tears and painful emotions, she would summon her attendants and ride home, in appearance and bearing still the Elfrida of her great days — the calm, proud-faced, beautiful woman who was once Edgar's queen.

XI

The time had arrived when Elfrida was deprived of this her one relief and consolation — her rides on the Downs and the exercise of her religion at the temple of the Great Stones — when in the second winter of her residence at Amesbury there fell a greater darkness than that of winter on England, when the pirate kings of the north began once more to frequent our shores, and the daily dreadful tale of battles and massacres and burning of villages and monasteries was heard throughout the kingdom. These invasions were at first confined to the eastern counties, but the agitation, with movements of men and outbreaks of lawlessness, were everywhere in the country, and the queen was warned that it was no longer safe for her to go out on Salisbury Plain.

The close seclusion in which she had now to live, confined to house and enclosed land, affected her spirits, and this was her darkest period, and it was also the turning-point in her life. For I now come to the strange story of her maid Editha, who, despite her humble position in the house, and albeit she was but a young girl in years, one, moreover, of a meek, timid disposition, was yet destined to play an exceedingly important part in the queen's history.

It happened that by chance or design the queen's maid, who was her closest attendant, who dressed and undressed her, was suddenly called away on some urgent matter, and this girl Editha, a stranger to all, was put in her place. The queen, who was in a moody and irritable state, presently discovered that the sight and presence of this girl produced a soothing effect on her darkened mind. She began to notice her when the maid combed her hair, when sitting with half-closed eyes in profound dejection she first looked attentively at that face behind her head in the mirror and marvelled at its fairness, the perfection of its lines and its delicate colouring, the pale gold hair and strangely serious grey eyes that were never lifted to meet her own.

What was it in this face, she asked herself, that held her and gave some rest to her tormented spirit? It reminded her of that crystal stream of sweet and bitter memories, at Wherwell, on which she used to gaze and in which she used to dip her hands, then to press the wetted hands to her lips. It also reminded her of an early morning sky, seen beyond and above the green dew-wet earth, so infinitely far away, so peaceful with a peace that was not of this earth.

It was not then merely its beauty that made this face so much to her, but something greater behind it, some inner grace, the peace of God in her soul.

One day there came for the queen as a gift from some distant town a volume of parables and fables for her entertainment. It was beautiful to the sight, being richly bound in silk and gold embroidery; but on opening it she soon found that there was little pleasure to be got from it on account of the difficulty she found in reading the crabbed handwriting. After spending some minutes in trying to decipher a paragraph or two she threw the book in disgust on the floor.

The maid picked it up, and after a glance at the first page said it was easy to her, and she asked if the queen would allow her to read it to her.

Elfrida, surprised, asked how it came about that her maid was able to read a difficult script with ease, or was able to read at all; and this was the first question she had condescended to put to the girl. Editha replied that she had been taught as a child by a great-uncle, a learned man; that she had been made to read volumes in a great variety of scripts to him, until reading had come easy to her, both Saxon and Latin.

Then, having received permission, she read the first fable aloud, and Elfrida listening, albeit without interest in the tale itself, found that the voice increased the girl's attraction for her. From that time the queen made her read to her every day. She would make her sit a little distance from her, and reclining on her couch, her head resting on her hand, she would let her eyes dwell on that sweet saint-like face until the reading was finished.

One day she read from the same book a tale of a great noble, an earldoman who was ruler under the king of that part of the country where his possessions were, whose power was practically unlimited and his word law. But he was a wise and just man, regardful of the rights of others, even of the meanest of men, so that he was greatly reverenced and loved by the people. Nevertheless, he too, like all men in authority, both good and bad, had his enemies, and the chief of these was a noble of a proud and froward temper who had quarrelled with him about their respective rights in certain properties where their lands adjoined. Again and again it was shown to him that his contention was wrong; the judgments against him only served to increase his bitterness and hostility until it seemed that there would never be an end to that strife. This at length so incensed his powerful overlord that he was forcibly deprived of his possessions and driven out beggared from his home. But no punishment, however severe, could change his nature; it only roused him to greater fury, a more fixed determination to have his revenge, so that outcast as he was his enmity was still to be feared and he was a danger to the ruler and the community in general. Then, at last, the great earl said he would suffer this state of things no longer, and he ordered his men to go out and seek and take him captive and bring him up for a final judgment. This was done, and the ruler then said he would not have him put to death as he was advised to do, so as to be rid of him once for all, but would inflict a greater punishment on him. He then made them put heavy irons on his ankles, riveted so that they should never be removed, and condemned him to slavery and to labour every day in his fields and pleasure-grounds for the rest of his life. To see his hated enemy reduced to that condition would, he said, be a satisfaction to him whenever he walked in his gardens.

These stern commands were obeyed, and when the miserable man refused to do his task and cried out in a rage that he would rather die, he was scourged until the blood ran from the wounds made by the lash; and at last, to escape from this torture, he was compelled to obey, and from morning to night he laboured on the land, planting and digging and doing whatever there was to do, always watched by his overseer, his food thrown to him as to a dog; laughed and jeered at by the meanest of the servants.

After a certain time, when his body grew hardened so that he could labour all day without pain, and, being fatigued, sleep all night without waking, though he had nothing but straw on a stone floor to lie upon; and when he was no longer mocked or punished or threatened with the lash, he began to reflect more and more on his condition, and to think that it would be possible to him to make it more endurable. When brooding on it, when he repined and cursed, it then seemed to him worse than death; but when, occupied with his task, he forgot that he was the slave of his enemy, who had overcome and broken him, then it no longer seemed so heavy. The sun still shone for him as for others; the earth was as green, the sky as blue, the flowers as fragrant. This reflection made his misery less; and by and by it came into his mind that it would be lessened more and more if he could forget that his master was his enemy and cruel persecutor, who took delight in the thought of his sufferings; if he could imagine that he had a different master, a great and good man who had ever been kind to him and whom his sole desire was to please. This thought working in his mind began to give him a satisfaction in his toil, and this change in him was noticed by his taskmaster, who began to see that he did his work with an understanding so much above that of his fellows that all those who laboured with him were influenced by his example, and whatsoever the toil was in which he had a part the work was better done. From the taskmaster this change became known to the chief head of all the lands, who thereupon had him set to other more important tasks, so that at last he was not only a toiler with pick and spade and pruning knife, but his counsel was sought in everything that concerned the larger works on the land; in forming plantations, in the draining of wet grounds and building of houses and bridges and the making of new roads. And in all these works he acquitted himself well.

Thus he laboured for years, and it all became known to the ruler, who at length ordered the man to be brought before him to receive yet another final judgment. And when he stood before him, hairy, dirty and unkempt, in his ragged raiment, with toil-hardened hands and heavy irons on his legs, he first ordered the irons to be removed.

The smiths came with their files and hammers, and with much labour took them off.

Then the ruler, his powerful old enemy, spoke these words to him: I do not know what your motives were in doing what you have done in all these years of your slavery; nor do I ask to be told. It is sufficient for me to know you have done these things, which are for my benefit and are a debt which must now be paid. You are henceforth free, and the possessions you were deprived of shall be restored to you, and as to the past and all the evil thoughts you had of me and all you did against me, it is forgiven and from this day will be forgotten. Go now in peace.

When this last word had been spoken by his enemy, all that remained of the old hatred and bitterness went out of him, and it was as if his soul as well as his feet had been burdened with heavy irons and that they had now been removed, and that he was free with a freedom he had never known before.

When the reading was finished, the queen with eyes cast down remained for some time immersed in thought; then with a keen glance at the maid's face she asked for the book, and opening it began slowly turning the leaves. By and by her face darkened, and in a stern tone of voice she said: Come here and show me in this book the parable you have just read, and then you shall also show me two or three other parables you have read to me on former occasions, which I cannot find.

The maid, pale and trembling, came and dropped on her knees and begged forgiveness for having recited these three or four tales, which she had heard or read elsewhere and committed to memory, and had pretended to read them out of the book.

Then the queen in a sudden rage said: Go from me and let me not see you again if you do not wish to be stripped and scourged and thrust naked out of the gates! And you only escape this punishment because the deceit you have been practising on me is, to my thinking, not of your own invention, but that of some crafty monk who is making you his instrument.

Editha, terrified and weeping, hurriedly quitted the room.

By and by, when that sudden tempest of rage had subsided, the despondence, which had been somewhat lightened by the maid's presence, came back on her so heavily that it was almost past endurance. She rose and went to her sleeping-room, and knelt before a table on which stood a crucifix with an image of the Saviour on it — the emblem of the religion she had so great a quarrel with. But not to pray. Folding her arms on the table and dropping her face on them she said: What have I done? And again and again she repeated: What have I done? Was it indeed a monk who taught her this deceit, or some higher being who put it in her mind to whisper a hope to my soul? To show me a way of escape from everlasting death — to labour in his fields and pleasure-grounds, a wretched slave with irons on her feet, to be scourged and mocked at, and in this state to cast out hatred and bitterness from my own soul and all remembrance of the injuries he had inflicted on me — to teach myself through long miserable years that this powerful enemy and persecutor is a kind and loving master? This is the parable, and now my soul tells me it would be a light punishment when I look at the red stains on these hands, and when the image of the boy I loved and murdered comes back to me. This then was the message, and I drove the messenger from me with cruel threats and insult.

Suddenly she rose, and going hurriedly out, called to her maids to bring Editha to her. They told her the maid had departed instantly on being dismissed, and had gone upwards of an hour. Then she ordered them to go and search for her in all the neighbourhood, at every house, and when they had found her to bring her back by persuasion or by force.

They returned after a time only to say they had sought for her everywhere and had failed to find or hear any report of her, but that some of the mounted men who had gone to look for her on the roads had not yet returned.

Left alone once more she turned to a window which looked towards Salisbury, and saw the westering sun hanging low in a sky of broken clouds over the valley of the Avon and the green downs on either side. And, still communing with herself, she said: I know that I shall not endure it long — this great fear of God — I know that it will madden me. And for the unforgiven who die mad there can be no hope. Only the sight of my maid's face with God's peace in it could save me from madness. No, I shall not go mad! I shall take it as a sign that I cannot be forgiven if the sun goes down without my seeing her again. I shall kill myself before madness comes and rest oblivious of life and all things, even of God's wrath, until the dreadful waking.

For some time longer she continued standing motionless, watching the sun, now sinking behind a dark cloud, then emerging and lighting up the dim interior of her room and her stone-white, desolate face.

Then once more her servants came back, and with them Editha, who had been found on the road to Salisbury, halfway there.

Left alone together, the queen took the maid by the hand and led her to a seat, then fell on her knees before her and clasped her legs and begged her forgiveness. When the maid replied that she had forgiven her, and tried to raise her up, she resisted, and cried: No, I cannot rise from my knees nor loose my hold on you until I have confessed to you and you have promised to save me. Now I see in you not my maid who combs my hair and ties my shoe-strings, but one that God loves, whom he exalts above the queens and nobles of the earth, and while I cling to you he will not strike. Look into this heart that has hated him, look at its frightful passions, its blood-guiltiness, and have compassion on me! And if you, O Editha, should reply to me that it is his will, for he has said it, that every soul shall save itself, show me the way. How shall I approach him? Teach me humility!

Thus she pleaded and abased herself. Nevertheless it was a hard task she imposed upon her helper, seeing that humility, of all virtues, was the most contrary to her nature. And when she was told that the first step to be taken was to be reconciled to the church, and to the head of the church, her chief enemy and persecutor, whose monks, obedient to his command, had blackened her name in all the land, her soul was in fierce revolt. Nevertheless she had to submit, seeing that God himself through his Son when on earth and his Son's disciples had established the church, and by that door only could any soul approach him. So there was an end to that conflict, and Elfrida, beaten and broken, although ever secretly hating the tonsured keepers of her soul, set forth under their guidance on her weary pilgrimage — the long last years of her bitter expiation.

Yet there was to be one more conflict between the two women — the imperious mistress and the humble-minded maid. This was when Editha announced to the other that the time had now come for her to depart. But the queen wished to keep her, and tried by all means to do so, by pleading with her and by threatening to detain her by force. Then repenting her anger and remembering the great debt of gratitude owing to the girl, she resolved to reward her generously, to bestow wealth on her, but in such a form that it would appear to the girl as a beautiful parting gift from one who had loved her: only afterwards, when they were far apart, would she discover its real value.

A memory of the past had come to her — of that day, sixteen years ago, when her lover came to her and using sweet flattering words poured out from a bag a great quantity of priceless jewels into her lap, and of the joy she had in the gift. Also how from the day of Athelwold's death she had kept those treasures put away in the same bag out of her sight. Nor in all the days of her life with Edgar had she ever worn a gem, though she had always loved to array herself magnificently, but her ornaments had been gold only, the work of the best artists in Europe. Now, in imitation of Athelwold, when his manner of bestowing the jewels had so charmed her, she would bestow them on the girl.

Accordingly when the moment of separation came and Editha was made to seat herself, the queen standing over her with the bag in her hand said: Do you, Editha, love all beautiful things? And when the maid had replied that she did, the other said: Then take these gems, which are beautiful, as a parting gift from me. And with that she poured out the mass of glittering jewels into the girl's lap.

But the maid without touching or even looking at them, and with a cry, I want no jewels! started to her feet so that they were all scattered upon the floor.

The queen stared astonished at the face before her with its new look of pride and excitement, then with rising anger she said: Is my maid too proud then to accept a gift from me? Does she not know that a single one of those gems thrown on the floor would be more than a fortune to her?

The girl replied in the same proud way: I am not your maid, and gems are no more to me than pebbles from the brook!

Then all at once recovering her meek, gentle manner she cried in a voice that pierced the queen's heart: O, not your maid, only your fellow-worker in our Master's fields and pleasure-grounds! Before I ever beheld your face, and since we have been together, my heart has bled for you, and my daily cry to God has been: Forgive her! Forgive her, for his sake who died for our sins! And this shall I continue to cry though I shall see you no more on earth. But we shall meet again. Not, O unhappy queen, at life's end, but long afterwards — long, long years! long ages!

Dropping on her knees she caught and kissed the queen's hand, shedding abundant tears on it, then rose and was quickly gone.

Elfrida, left to herself, scarcely recovered from the shock of surprise at that sudden change in the girl's manner, began to wonder at her own blindness in not having seen through her disguise from the first. The revelation had come to her only at the last moment in that proud gesture and speech when her gift was rejected, not without scorn. A child of nobles great as any in the land, what had made her do this thing? What indeed but the heavenly spirit that was in her, the spirit that was in Christ — the divine passion to save!

Now she began to ponder on those last words the maid had spoken, and the more she thought of them the greater became her sadness until it was like the approach of death. O terrible words! Yet it was what she had feared, even when she had dared to hope for forgiveness. Now she knew what her life after death was to be since the word had been spoken by those inspired lips. O dreadful destiny! To dwell alone, to tread alone that desert desolate, that illimitable waste of burning sand stretching from star to star through infinite space, where was no rock nor tree to give her shade, no fountain to quench her fiery thirst! For that was how she imaged the future life, as a desert to be dwelt in until in the end, when in God's good time — the time of One to whom a thousand years are as one day — she would receive the final pardon and be admitted to rest in a green and shaded place.

Overcome with the agonising thought she sank down on her couch and fell into a faint. In that state she was found by her women, reclining, still as death, with eyes closed, the whiteness of death in her face; and thinking her dead they rushed out terrified, crying aloud and lamenting that the queen was dead.

XII

She was not dead. She recovered from that swoon, but never from the deep, unbroken sadness caused by those last words of the maid Editha, which had overcome and nearly slain her. She now abandoned her seclusion, but the world she returned to was not the old one. The thought that every person she met was saying in his or her heart: This is Elfrida; this is the queen who murdered Edward the Martyr, her step-son, made that world impossible. The men and women she now consorted with were the religious and ecclesiastics of all degrees, and abbots and abbesses. These were the people she loved least, yet now into their hands she deliberately gave herself; and to those who questioned her, to her spiritual guides, she revealed all her life and thoughts and passions, opening her soul to their eyes like a manuscript for them to read and consider; and when they told her that in God's sight she was guilty of the murder both of Edward and Athelwold, she replied that they doubtless knew best what was in God's mind, and whatever they commanded her to do that should be done, and if in her own mind it was not as they said this could be taken as a defect in her understanding. For in her heart she was not changed, and had not yet and never would learn the bitter lesson of humility. Furthermore, she knew better than they what life and death had in store for her, since it had been revealed to her by holier lips than those of any priest. Lips on which had been laid a coal from the heavenly altar, and what they had foretold would come to pass — that unearthly pilgrimage and purification — that destiny, dreadful, ineluctable, that made her soul faint to think of it. Here, on this earth, it was for her to toil, a slave with heavy irons on her feet, in her master's fields and pleasure-grounds, and these gowned men with shaven heads, wearing ropes of beads and crucifixes as emblems of their authority — these were the taskmasters set over her, and to these, she, Elfrida, one time queen in England, would bend in submission and humbly confess her sins, and uncomplainingly take whatever austerities or other punishments they decreed.

Here, then, at Amesbury itself, she began her works of expiation, and found that she, too, like the unhappy man in the parable, could experience some relief and satisfaction in her solitary embittered existence in the work itself.

Having been told that at this village where she was living a monastery had existed and had been destroyed in the dreadful wars of two to three centuries ago, she conceived the idea of founding a new one, a nunnery, and endowing it richly, and accordingly the Abbey of Amesbury was built and generously endowed by her.

This religious house became famous in after days, and was resorted to by the noblest ladies in the land who desired to take the veil, including princesses and widow queens; and it continued to flourish for centuries, down to the Dissolution.

This work completed, she returned, after nineteen years, to her old home at Wherwell. Since she had lost sight of her maid Editha, she had been possessed with a desire to re-visit that spot, where she had been happy as a young bride and had repined in solitude and had had her glorious triumph and stained her soul with crime. She craved for it again, especially to look once more at the crystal current of the Test in which she had been accustomed to dip her hands. The grave, saintly face of Editha had reminded her of that stream; and Editha she might not see. She could not seek for her, nor speak to her, nor cry to her to come back to her, since she had said that they would meet no more on earth.

Having become possessed of the castle which she had

once regarded as her prison and cage, she ordered its demolition and used the materials in building the abbey she founded at that spot, and it was taken for granted by the Church that this was done in expiation of the part she had taken in Athelwold's murder. At this spot where the stream became associated in her mind with the thought of Editha, and was a sacred stream, she resolved to end her days. But the time of her retirement was not yet, there was much still waiting for her to do in her master's fields and pleasure-grounds. For no sooner had the tidings of her work in founding these monasteries and the lavish use she was making of her great wealth been spread abroad, than from many religious houses all over the land the cry was sent to her — the Macedonian cry to St. Paul to come over and help us.

From the houses founded by Edgar the cry was particularly loud and insistent. There were forty-seven of them, and had not Edgar died so soon there would have been fifty, that being the number he had set his heart on in his fervid zeal for religion. All, alas! were insufficiently endowed; and it was for Elfrida, as they were careful to point out, to increase their income from her great wealth, seeing that this would enable them to associate her name with that of Edgar and keep it in memory, and this would be good for her soul.

To all such calls she listened, and she performed many and long journeys to the religious houses all over the country to look closely into their conditions and needs, and to all she gave freely or in moderation, but not always without a gesture of scorn. For in her heart of hearts she was still Elfrida and unchanged, albeit outwardly she had attained to humility; only once during these years of travel and toil when she was getting rid of her wealth did she allow her secret bitterness and hostility to her ecclesiastical guides and advisers to break out.

She was at Worcester, engaged in a conference with the

bishop and several of his clergy; they were sitting at an oak table with some papers and plans before them, when the news was brought into the room that Archbishop Dunstan was dead.

They all, except Elfrida, started to their feet with the looks and exclamations of dismay, as if some frightful calamity had come to pass. Then dropping to their knees with bowed heads and lifted hands they prayed for the repose of his soul. They prayed silently, but the silence was broken by a laugh from the queen. Starting to his feet the bishop turned on her a severe countenance, and asked why she laughed at that solemn moment.

She replied that she had laughed unthinkingly, as the linnet sings, from pure joy of heart at the glad tidings that their holy archbishop had been translated to paradise. For if he had done so much for England when burdened with the flesh, how much more would he be able to do now from the seat or throne to which he would be exalted in heaven in virtue of the position his blessed mother now occupied in that place.

The bishop, angered at her mocking words, turned his back on her, and the others, following his example, averted their faces, but not one word did they utter.

They remembered that Dunstan in former years, when striving to make himself all powerful in the kingdom, had made free use of a supernatural machinery; that when he wanted something done and it could not be done in any other way, he received a command from heaven, brought to him by some saint or angel, to have it done, and the command had then to be obeyed. They also remembered that when Dunstan, as he informed them, had been snatched up into the seventh heaven, he did not on his return to earth modestly, like St. Paul, that it was not lawful for him to speak of the things which he had heard and seen, but he proclaimed them to an astonished world in his loudest trumpet voice. Also, that when, by these means, he had established his power and influence and knew that he could trust his own subtle brains to maintain his position, he had dropped the miracles and visions. And it had come to pass that when the archbishop had seen fit to leave the supernatural element out of his policy, the heads of the Church in England were only too pleased to have it so. The world had gaped with astonishment at these revelations long enough, and its credulity had come near to the breaking point, on which account the raking up of these perilous matters by the queen was fiercely resented.

But the queen was not yet satisfied that enough had been said by her. Now she was in full revolt she must give out once for all the hatred of her old enemy, which his death had not appeased.

What mean you, Fathers, she cried, by turning your backs on me and keeping silence? Is it an insult to me you intend or to the memory of that great and holy man who has just quitted the earth? Will you dare to say that the reports he brought to us of the marvellous doings he witnessed in heaven, when he was taken there, were false and the lies and inventions of Satan, whose servant he was?

More than that she was not allowed to say, for now the bishop in a mighty rage swung round, and dealt a blow on the table with such fury that his arm was disabled by it, he shouted at her: Not another word! Hold your mocking tongue, fiendish woman! Then plucking up his gown with his left hand for fear of being tripped up by it he rushed out of the room.

The others, still keeping their faces averted from her, followed at a more dignified pace; and seeing them depart she cried after them: Go, Fathers, and tell your bishop that if he had not run away so soon he would have been rewarded for his insolence by a slap in the face.

This outburst on her part caused no lasting break in her

relations with the Church. It was to her merely an incident in her long day's toil in her master's fields — a quarrel she had had with an overseer; while he, on his side, even before he recovered the use of his injured arm, thought it best for their souls, as well as for the interests of the Church, to say no more about it. Her great works of expiation were accordingly continued. But the time at length arrived for her to take her long-desired rest before facing the unknown dreaded future. She was not old in years, but remorse and a deep settled melancholy and her frequent fierce wrestlings with her own rebellious nature as with an untamed dangerous animal chained to her had made her old. Furthermore, she had by now well-nigh expended all her possessions and wealth, even to the gems she had once prized and then thrust away out of sight for many years, and which her maid Editha had rejected with scorn, saying they were no more to her than pebbles from the brook.

Once more at Wherwell, she entered the Abbey, and albeit she took the veil herself she was not under the same strict rule as her sister nuns. The Abbess herself retired to Winchester and ruled the convent from that city, while Elfrida had the liberty she desired, to live and do as she liked in her own rooms and attend prayers and meals only when inclined to do so. There, as always, since Edward's death, her life was a solitary one, and in the cold season she would have her fire of logs and sit before it as in the old days in the castle, brooding ever on her happy and unhappy past and on the awful future, the years and centuries of suffering and purification.

It was chiefly this thought of the solitariness of that future state, that companionless way, centuries long, that daunted her. Here in this earthly state, darkened as it was, there were yet two souls she could and constantly did hold communion with — Editha still on earth, though not with her, and Edward in heaven; but in that dreadful desert to which she would be banished there would be a great gulf set between her soul and theirs.

But perhaps there would be others she had known, whose lives had been interwoven with hers, she would be allowed to commune with in that same place. Edgar of a certainty would be there, although Glastonbury had built him a chapel and put him in a silver tomb and had begun to call him Saint Edgar. Would he find her and seek to have speech with her? It was anguish to her even to think of such an encounter. She would say, Do not come to me, for rather would I be alone in this dreadful solitude for a thousand years than have you, Edgar, for company. For I have not now one thought or memory of you in my soul that is not bitter. It is true that I once loved you: even before I saw your face I loved you, and said in my heart that we two were destined to be one. And my love increased when we were united, and you gave me my heart's desire — the power I loved, and glory in the sight of the world. And although in my heart I laughed at your pretended zeal for a pure religion while you were gratifying your lower desires and chasing after fair women all over the land, I admired and gloried in your nobler qualities, your activity and vigilance in keeping the peace within your borders, and in making England master of the seas, so that the pirate kings of the North ventured not to approach our shores. But on your own gross appetites you would put no restraint, but gave yourself up to wine and gluttony and made a companion of Death, even in the flower of your age you were playing with Death, and when you had lived but half your years you rode away with Death and left me alone; you, Edgar, the mighty hunter and slayer of wolves, you rode away and left me to the wolves, alone, in a dark forest. Therefore the guilt of Edward's death is yours more than mine, though my soul is stained red with his blood, seeing that you left me to fight alone, and in my madness, not knowing what I did, I stained myself with this crime.

But what you have done to me is of little moment, seeing that mine is but one soul of the many thousands that were given into your keeping, and your crime in wasting your life for the sake of base pleasures was committed against an entire nation, and not of the living only but also the great and glorious dead of the race of Cerdic — of the men who have laboured these many centuries, shedding their blood on a hundred stricken fields, to build up this kingdom of England; and when their mighty work was completed it was given into your hands to keep and guard. And you died and abandoned it; Death, your playmate, has taken you away, and Edgar's peace is no more. Now your ships are scattered or sunk in the sea, now the invaders are again on your coasts as in the old dreadful days, burning and slaying, and want is everywhere and fear is in all hearts throughout the land. And the king, your son, who inherited your beautiful face and nought beside except your vices and whatever was least worthy of a king, he too is now taking his pleasure, even as you took yours, in a gay bejewelled dress, with some shameless woman at his side and a wine-cup in his hand. O unhappy mother that I am, that I must curse the day a son was born to me! O grief immitigable that it was my deed, my dreadful deed, that raised him to the throne — the throne that was Alfred's and Edmund's and Athelstan's!

These were the thoughts that were her only company as she sat brooding before her winter fire, day after day, and winter following winter, while the years deepened the lines of anguish on her face and whitened the hair that was once red gold.

But in the summer time she was less unhappy, for then she could spend the long hours out of doors under the sky in the large shaded gardens of the convent with the stream for boundary on the lower side. This stream had now become more to her than in the old days when, languishing in solitude, she had made it a companion and confidant. For now it had become associated in her mind with the image of the maid Editha, and when she sat again at the old spot on the bank gazing on the swift crystal current, then dipping her hand in it and putting the wetted hand to her lips, the stream and Editha were one.

Then one day she was missed, and for a long time they sought for her all through the building and in the grounds without finding her. Then the seekers heard a loud cry, and saw one of the nuns running towards the convent door, with her hands pressed to her face as if to shut out some dreadful sight; and when they called to her she pointed back towards the stream and ran on to the house. Then all the sisters who were out in the grounds hurried down to the stream to the spot where Elfrida was accustomed to sit, and were horrified to see her lying drowned in the water.

It was a hot, dry summer and the stream was low, and in stooping to dip her hand in the water she had lost her balance and fallen in, and although the water was but three feet deep she had in her feebleness been unable to save herself. She was lying on her back on the clearly seen bed of many-coloured pebbles, her head pointing downstream, and the swift fretting current had carried away her hood and pulled out her long abundant silver-white hair, and the current played with her hair, now pulling it straight out, then spreading it wide over the surface, mixing its silvery threads with the hair-like green blades of the floating water-grass. And the dead face was like marble; but the wide-open eyes that had never wholly lost their brilliance and the beautiful lungwort blue colour were like living eyes — living and gazing through the crystal-clear running water at the group of nuns staring down with horror-struck faces at her.

Thus ended Elfrida's darkened life; nor did it seem an

unfit end; for it was as if she had fallen into the arms of the maiden who had in her thoughts become one with the stream — the saintly Editha through whose sacrifice and intercession she had been saved from death everlasting.

AN OLD THORN

I

The little village of Ingden lies in a hollow of the South Wiltshire Downs, the most isolated of the villages in that lonely district. Its one short street is crossed at right angles in the middle part by the Salisbury road, and standing just at that point, the church on one hand, the old inn on the other, you can follow it with the eye for a distance of nearly three miles. First it goes winding up the low down under which the village stands, then vanishes over the brow to reappear again a mile and a half further away as a white band on the vast green slope of the succeeding down, which rises to a height of over 600 feet. On the summit it vanishes once more, but those who use it know it for a laborious road crossing several high ridges before dropping down into the valley road leading to Salisbury.

When, standing in the village street, your eye travels up that white band, you can distinctly make out even at that distance a small, solitary tree standing near the summit — an old thorn with an ivy growing on it. My walks were often that way, and invariably on coming to that point I would turn twenty yards aside from the road to spend half an hour seated on the turf near or under the old tree. These half-hours were always grateful; and conscious that the tree drew me to it I questioned myself as to the reason. It was, I told myself, nothing but mental curiosity: my interest was a purely scientific one. For how comes it, I asked, that a thorn can grow to a tree and live to a great age in such a situation, on a vast, naked down, where for many centuries, perhaps for thousands of years, the herbage has been so closely fed by sheep as to have the appearance of a carpet, or newly mown lawn? The seed is carried and scattered everywhere by the birds, but no sooner does it germinate and send up a shoot than it is eaten down to the roots; for there is no scent that attracts a sheep more, no flavour it has greater taste for, than that of any forest seedling springing up amidst the minute herbaceous plants which carpet the downs. The thorn, like other organisms, has its own unconscious intelligence and cunning, by means of which it endeavours to save itself and fulfil its life. It opens its first tender leaves under the herbage, and at the same time thrusts up a vertical spine to wound the nibbling mouth; and no sooner has it got a leaf or two and a spine than it spreads its roots all round, and from each of them springs a fresh shoot, leaves and protecting spine, to increase the chances of preservation. In vain! the cunning animal finds a way to defeat all this strategy, and after the leaves have been bitten off again and again, the infant plant gives up the struggle and dies in the ground. Yet we see that from time to time one survives — one perhaps in a million; but how — whether by a quicker growth or a harder or more poisonous thorn, an unpalatable leaf, or some other secret agency — we cannot guess. First as a diminutive scrubby shrub, with numerous iron-hard stems, with few and small leaves but many thorns, it keeps its poor flowerless frustrate life for perhaps half a century or longer, without growing more than a couple of feet high; and then, as by a miracle, it will spring up until its top shoots are out of reach of the browsing sheep, and in the end it becomes a tree with spreading branches and fully developed leaves, and flowers and fruit in their season.

One day I was visited by an artist from a distance who, when shown the thorn, pronounced it a fine subject for his pencil, and while he made his picture we talked about the hawthorn generally as compared with other trees, and agreed that, except in its blossoming time when it is merely pretty, it is the most engaging and perhaps the most beautiful of our native trees. We said that it was the most *individual* of trees, that its variety was infinite, for you never find two alike, whether growing in a forest, in groups, or masses, or alone. We were almost lyrical in its praises. But the solitary thorn was always best, he said, and this one was perhaps the best of all he had seen: strange and at the same time decorative in its form, beautiful too in its appearance of great age with unimpaired vigour and something more in its expression — that elusive something which we find in some trees and don't know how to explain.

Ah, yes, thought I, it was this appeal to the æsthetic faculty which attracted me from the first, and not, as I had imagined, the mere curiosity of the naturalist interested mainly and always in the *habits* of living things, plant or animal.

Certainly the thorn had strangeness. Its appearance as to height was deceptive; one would have guessed it eighteen feet; measuring it I was surprised to find it only ten. It has four separate boles, springing from one root, leaning a little away from each other, the thickest just a foot in circumference. The branches are few, beginning at about five feet from the ground, the foliage thin, the leaves throughout the summer stained with grey, rust-red, and purple colour. Though so small and exposed to the full fury of every wind that blows over that vast naked down, it has yet an ivy growing on it — the strangest of the many strange ivy-plants I have seen. It comes out of the ground as two ivy trunks on opposite sides of the stoutest bole, but at a height of four feet from the surface the two join and ascend the tree as one round iron-coloured and iron-hard stem, which goes curving and winding snakewise among the branches as if with the object of roping them to save them from being torn off by the winds. Finally, rising to the top, the long serpent stem opens out in a flat disc-shaped mass of close-packed branchlets and twigs densely set with small round leaves, dark dull green and tough as parchment. One could only suppose that thorn and ivy had been partners from the beginning of life, and that the union was equally advantageous to both.

The small ivy disc or platform on top of the tree was a favourite stand and look-out for the downland birds. I seldom visited the spot without disturbing some of them, now a little company of missel-thrushes, now a crowd of starlings, then perhaps a dozen rooks, crowded together, looking very big and conspicuous on their little platform.

Being curious to find out something about the age of the tree, I determined to put the question to my old friend Malachi, aged eighty-nine, who was born and had always lived in the parish and had known the downs and probably every tree growing on them for miles around from his earliest years. It was my custom to drop in of an evening and sit with him, listening to his endless reminiscences of his young days. That evening I spoke of the thorn, describing its position and appearance, thinking that perhaps he had forgotten it. How long, I asked him, had the thorn been there?

He was one of those men, usually of the labouring class, to be met with in such lonely, out-of-the-world places as the Wiltshire Downs, whose eyes never look old however many their years may be, and are more like the eyes of a bird or animal than a human being, for they gaze at you and through you when you speak without appearing to know what you say. So it was on this occasion; he looked straight at me with no sign of understanding, no change in his clear grey eyes, and answered nothing. But I would not be put off, and when, raising my voice, I repeated the question, he replied, after another interval of silence, that the thorn "was never any different." 'Twas just the same, ivy and all, when he were a small boy. It looked just so old; why, he remembered his old father saying the same thing — 'twas the same when he were a boy, and 'twas the same in his father's time. Then anxious to escape from the subject he began talking of something else.

It struck me that after all the most interesting thing about the thorn was its appearance of great age, and this aspect I had now been told had continued for at least a century, probably for a much longer time. It produced a reverent feeling in me such as we experience at the sight of some ancient stone monument. But the tree was alive, and because of its life the feeling was perhaps stronger than in the case of a granite cross or cromlech or other memorial of antiquity.

Sitting by the thorn one day it occurred to me that, growing at this spot close to the road and near the summit of that vast down, numberless persons travelling to and from Salisbury must have turned aside to rest on the turf in the shade after that laborious ascent or before beginning the long descent to the valley below. Travellers of all conditions, on foot or horseback, in carts and carriages, merchants, bagmen, farmers, drovers, gipsies, tramps and vagrants of all descriptions, and from time to time troops of soldiers. Yet never one of them had injured the tree in any way! I could not remember ever finding a tree growing alone by the roadside in a lonely place which had not the marks of many old and new wounds inflicted on its trunk with knives, hatchets, and other implements. Here not a mark, not a scratch had been made on any one of its four trunks or on the ivy stem by any thoughtless or mischievous person, nor had any branch been cut or broken off. Why had they one and all respected this tree?

It was another subject to talk to Malachi about, and to him I went after tea and found him with three of his neighbours sitting by the fire and talking; for though it was summer the old man always had a fire in the evening.

They welcomed and made room for me, but I had no sooner broached the subject in my mind than they all fell into silence, then after a brief interval the three callers began to discuss some little village matter. I was not going to be put off in that way, and, leaving them out, went on talking to Malachi about the tree. Presently one by one the three visitors got up and, remarking that it was time to be going, they took their departure.

The old man could not escape nor avoid listening, and in the end had to say something. He said he didn't know nothing about all them tramps and gipsies and other sorts of men who had sat by the tree; all he knowed was that the old thorn had been a good thorn to him — first and last. He remembered once when he was a young man, not yet twenty, he went to do some work at a village five miles away, and being winter time he left early, about four o'clock, to walk home over the downs. He had just got married, and had promised his wife to be home for tea at six o'clock. But a thick fog came up over the downs, and soon as it got dark he lost himself. 'Twas the darkest, thickest night he had ever been out in; and whenever he came against a bank or other obstruction he would get down on his hands and knees and feel it up and down to get its shape and find out what it was, for he knew all the marks on his native downs; 'twas all in vain — nothing could he recognise. In this way he wandered about for hours, and was in despair of getting home that night, when all at once there came a sense of relief, a feeling that it was all right, that something was guiding him.

I remarked that I knew what that meant: he had lost his sense of direction and had now all at once recovered it; such a thing had often happened; I once had such an experience myself.

No, it was not that, he returned. He had not gone a dozen steps from the moment that sense of confidence came to him, before he ran into a tree, and feeling the trunk with his hands he recognised it as the old thorn and knew where he was. In a couple of minutes he was on the road, and in less than an hour, just about midnight, he was safe at home.

No more could I get out of him, at all events on that occasion; nor did I ever succeed in extracting any further personal experience in spite of his having let out that the thorn had been a good thorn to him, first and last. I had, however, heard enough to satisfy me that I had at length discovered the real secret of the tree's fascination. I recalled other trees which had similarly affected me, and how, long years ago, when a good deal of my time was spent on horseback, whenever I found myself in a certain district I would go miles out of my way just to look at a solitary old tree growing in a lonely place, and to sit for an hour to refresh myself, body and soul, in its shade. I had indeed all along suspected the thorn of being one of this order of mysterious trees; and from other experiences I had met with, one some years ago in a village in this same county of Wilts, I had formed the opinion that in many persons the sense of a strange intelligence and possibility of power in such trees is not a mere transitory state but an enduring influence which profoundly affects their whole lives.

Determined to find out something more, I went to other villagers, mostly women, who are more easily disarmed and made to believe that you too know and are of the same mind with them, being under the same mysterious power and spell. In this way, laying many a subtle snare, I succeeded in eliciting a good deal of information. It was, however, mostly of a kind which could not profitably be used in any inquiry into the subject; it simply went to show that the feeling existed and was strong in many of the villagers. During this inquiry I picked up several anecdotes about a person who lived in Ingden close upon three generations ago, and was able to piece them together so as to make a consistent narrative of his life. This was Johnnie Budd, a farm labourer, who came to his end in 1821, a year or so before my old friend Malachi was born. It is going very far back, but there were circumstances in his life which made a deep impression on the mind of that little community, and the story had lived on through all these years.

II

Johnnie had fallen on hard times when in an exceptionally severe winter season he with others had been thrown out of employment at the farm where he worked; then with a wife and three small children to keep he had in his desperation procured food for them one dark night in an adjacent field. But alas! one of the little ones playing in the road with some of her companions, who were all very hungry, let it out that she wasn't hungry, that for three days she had had as much nice meat as she wanted to eat! Play over, the hungry little ones flew home to tell their parents the wonderful news — why didn't they have nice meat like Tilly Budd, instead of a piece of rye bread without even dripping on it, when they were so hungry? Much talk followed, and spread from cottage to cottage until it reached the constable's ears, and he, already informed of the loss of a wether taken from its fold close by, went straight to Johnnie and charged him with the offence. Johnnie lost his head, and dropping on his knees confessed his guilt and begged his old friend Lampard to have mercy on him and to overlook it for the sake of his wife and children.

It was his first offence, but when he was taken from the lock-up at the top of the village street to be conveyed to Salisbury, his friends and neighbours who had gathered at the spot to witness his removal shook their heads and doubted that Ingden would ever see him again. The confession had made the case so simple a one that he had at once been committed to take his trial at the Salisbury Assizes, and as the time was near the constable had been ordered to convey the prisoner to the town himself. Accordingly he engaged old Joe Blaskett, called Daddy in the village, to take them in his pony cart. Daddy did not want the job, but was talked or bullied into it, and there he now sat in his cart, waiting in glum silence for his passengers; a bent old man of eighty, with a lean, grey, bitter face, in his rusty cloak, his old rabbit-skin cap drawn down over his ears, his white disorderly beard scattered over his chest. The constable Lampard was a big, powerful man, with a great round, good-natured face, but just now he had a strong sense of responsibility, and to make sure of not losing his prisoner he handcuffed him before bringing him out and helping him to take his seat on the bottom of the cart. Then he got up himself to his seat by the driver's side; the last good-bye was spoken, the weeping wife being gently led away by her friends, and the cart rattled away down the street. Turning into the Salisbury road it was soon out of sight over the near down, but half an hour later it emerged once more into sight beyond the great dip, and the villagers who had remained standing about at the same spot watched it crawling like a beetle up the long white road on the slope of the vast down beyond.

Johnnie was now lying coiled up on his rug, his face hidden between his arms, abandoned to grief, sobbing aloud. Lampard, sitting athwart the seat so as to keep an eye on him, burst out at last: "Be a man, Johnnie, and stop your crying! 'Tis making things no better by taking on like that. What do you say, Daddy?"

"I say nought," snapped the old man, and for a while they proceeded in silence except for those heartrending sobs. As they approached the old thorn tree, near the top of the long slope, Johnnie grew more and more agitated, his whole frame shaking with his sobbing. Again the constable rebuked him, telling him that 'twas a shame for a man to go on like that. Then with an effort he restrained his sobs, and lifting a red, swollen, tear-stained face he stammered out: "Master Lampard, did I ever ask 'ee a favour in my life?"

"What be after now?" said the other suspiciously. "Well,

no, Johnnie, not as I remember."

"An' do 'ee think I'll ever come back home again, Master Lampard?"

"Maybe no, maybe yes; 'tis not for me to say."

"But 'ee knows 'tis a hanging matter?"

"'Tis that for sure. But you be a young man with a wife and childer, and have never done no wrong before — not that I ever heard say. Maybe the judge'll recommend you to mercy. What do you say, Daddy?"

The old man only made some inarticulate sounds in his beard, without turning his head.

"But, Master Lampard, suppose I don't swing, they'll send I over the water and I'll never see the wife and children no more."

"Maybe so; I'm thinking that's how 'twill be."

"Then will 'ee do me a kindness? 'Tis the only one I ever asked 'ee, and there'll be no chance to ask 'ee another."

"I can't say, Johnnie, not till I know what 'tis you want."

"'Tis only this, Master Lampard. When we git to th' old thorn let me out o' the cart and let me stand under it one minnit and no more."

"Be you wanting to hang yourself before the trial then?" said the constable, trying to make a joke of it.

"I couldn't do that," said Johnnie, simply, "seeing my hands be fast and you'd be standing by."

"No, no, Johnnie, 'tis nought but just foolishness. What do you say, Daddy?"

The old man turned round with a look of sudden rage in his grey face which startled Lampard; but he said nothing, he only opened and shut his mouth two or three times without a sound.

Meanwhile the pony had been going slower and slower for the last thirty or forty yards, and now when they were abreast of the tree stood still.

"What be stopping for?" cried Lampard. "Get on — get

on, or we'll never get to Salisbury this day."

Then at length old Blaskett found a voice.

"Does thee know what thee's saying, Master Lampard, or be thee a stranger in this parish?"

"What d'ye mean, Daddy? I be no stranger; I've a-known this parish and known 'ee these nine years."

"Thee asked why I stopped when 'twas the pony stopped, knowing where we'd got to. But thee's not born here or thee'd a-known what a hoss knows. An' since 'ee asks what I says, I say this, 'twill not hurt 'ee to let Johnnie Budd stand one minute by the tree."

Feeling insulted and puzzled the constable was about to assert his authority when he was arrested by Johnnie's cry, "Oh, Master Lampard, 'tis my last hope!" and by the sight of the agony of suspense on his swollen face. After a short hesitation he swung himself out over the side of the cart, and letting down the tailboard laid rough hands on Johnnie and half helped, half dragged him out.

They were quickly by the tree, where Johnnie stood silent with downcast eyes a few moments; then dropping upon his knees leant his face against the bark, his eyes closed, his lips murmuring.

"Time's up!" cried Lampard presently, and taking him by the collar pulled him to his feet; in a couple of minutes more they were in the cart and on their way.

It was grey weather, very cold, with an east wind blowing, but for the rest of that dreary thirteen-miles journey Johnnie was very quiet and submissive and shed no more tears.

III

What had been his motive in wishing to stand by the tree? What did he expect when he said it was his last hope? During the way up the long, laborious slope, an incident of his early years in connection with the tree had been in his mind, and had wrought on him until it culminated in that passionate outburst and his strange request. It was when he was a boy, not quite ten years old, that, one afternoon in the summer time, he went with other children to look for wild raspberries on the summit of the great down. Johnnie, being the eldest, was the leader of the little band. On the way back from the brambly place where the fruit grew, on approaching the thorn, they spied a number of rooks sitting on it, and it came into Johnnie's mind that it would be great fun to play at crows by sitting on the branches as near the top as they could get. Running on, with cries that sent the rooks cawing away, they began swarming up the trunks, but in the midst of their frolic, when they were all struggling for the best places on the branches, they were startled by a shout, and looking up to the top of the down, saw a man on horseback coming towards them at a gallop, shaking a whip in anger as he rode. Instantly they began scrambling down, falling over each other in their haste, then, picking themselves up, set off down the slope as fast as they could run. Johnnie was foremost, while close behind him came Marty, who was nearly the same age and, though a girl, almost as swift-footed, but before going fifty yards she struck her foot against an ant-hill and was thrown violently, face down, on the turf. Johnnie turned at her cry and flew back to help her up, but the shock of the fall, and her extreme terror, had deprived her for the moment of all strength, and while he struggled to raise her, the smaller children, one by one, overtook and passed them, and in another moment the man was off his horse, standing over them.

"Do you want a good thrashing?" he said, grasping Johnnie by the collar.

"Oh, sir; please don't hit me!" answered Johnnie; then looking up he was astonished to see that his captor was not the stern old farmer, the tenant of the down, he had taken him for, but a stranger and a strange-looking man, in a dark grey cloak with a red collar. He had a pointed beard and long black hair and dark eyes that were not evil yet frightened Johnnie, when he caught them gazing down on him.

"No, I'll not thrash you," said he, "because you stayed to help the little maiden, but I'll tell you something for your good about the tree you and your little mates have been climbing, bruising the bark with your heels and breaking off leaves and twigs. Do you know, boy, that if you hurt it, it will hurt you? It stands fast here with its roots in the ground and you — you can go away from it, you think. 'Tis not so; something will come out of it and follow you wherever you go and hurt and break you at last. But if you make it a friend and care for it, it will care for you and give you happiness and deliver you from evil."

Then touching Johnnie's cheeks with his gloved hand he got on his horse and rode away, and no sooner was he gone than Marty started up, and hand in hand the two children set off at a run down the long slope.

Johnnie's playtime was nearly over then, for by and by he was taken as farmer's boy at one of the village farms. When he was nineteen years old, one Sunday evening, when standing in the road with other young people of the village, youths and girls, it was powerfully borne on his mind that his old playmate Marty was not only the prettiest and best girl in the place, but that she had something which set her apart and far, far above all other women. For now, after having known her intimately from his first years, he had suddenly fallen in love with her, a feeling which caused him to shiver in a kind of ecstasy, yet made him miserable, since it had purged his sight and made him see, too, how far apart they were and how hopeless his case. It was true they had been comrades from childhood, fond of each other, but she had grown and developed until she had become that most bright and lovely being, while he had remained the same slow-witted, awkward, almost inarticulate Johnnie he had always been. This feeling preyed on his poor mind, and when he joined the evening gathering in the village street he noted bitterly how contemptuously he was left out of the conversation by the others, how incapable he was of keeping pace with them in their laughing talk and banter. And, worst of all, how Marty was the leading spirit, bandying words and bestowing smiles and pleasantries all round, but never a word or a smile for him. He could not endure it, and so instead of smartening himself up after work and going for company to the village street, he would walk down the secluded lane near the farm to spend the hour before supper and bedtime sitting on a gate, brooding on his misery; and if by chance he met Marty in the village he would try to avoid her, and was silent and uncomfortable in her presence.

After work, one hot summer evening, Johnnie was walking along the road near the farm in his working clothes, clay-coloured boots, and old dusty hat, when who should he see but Marty coming towards him, looking very sweet and fresh in her light-coloured print gown. He looked to this side and that for some friendly gap or opening in the hedge so as to take himself out of the road, but there was no way of escape at that spot, and he had to pass her, and so casting down his eyes he walked on, wishing he could sink into the earth out of her sight. But she would not allow him to pass; she put herself directly in his way and spoke.

"What's the matter with 'ee, Johnnie, that 'ee don't want to meet me and hardly say a word when I speak to 'ee?"

He could not find a word in reply; he stood still, his face crimson, his eyes on the ground.

"Johnnie, dear, what is it?" she asked, coming closer and putting her hand on his arm.

Then he looked up, and seeing the sweet compassion in her eyes, he could no longer keep the secret of his pain from her.

"'Tis 'ee, Marty," he said. "Thee'll never want I — there's others 'ee'll like better. 'Tisn't for I to say a word about that, I'm thinking, for I be — just nothing. An' — an' — I be going away from the village, Marty, and I'll never come back no more."

"Oh, Johnnie, don't 'ee say it! Would 'ee go and break my heart? Don't 'ee know I've always loved 'ee since we were little mites together?"

And thus it came about that Johnnie, most miserable of men, was all at once made happy beyond his wildest dreams. And he proved himself worthy of her; from that time there was not a more diligent and sober young labourer in the village, nor one of a more cheerful disposition, nor more careful of his personal appearance when, the day's work done, the young people had their hour of social intercourse and courting. Yet he was able to put by a portion of his weekly wages of six shillings to buy sticks, so that when spring came round again he was able to marry and take Marty to live with him in his own cottage.

One Sunday afternoon, shortly after this happy event, they went out for a walk on the high down.

"Oh, Johnnie, 'tis a long time since we were here together, not since we used to come and play and look for cowslips when we were little."

Johnnie laughed with pure joy and said they would just be children and play again, now they were alone and out of sight of the village; and when she smiled up at him he rejoiced to think that his union with this perfect girl was producing a happy effect on his poor brains, making him as bright and ready with a good reply as any one. And in their happiness they played at being children just as in the old days they had played at being grown-ups. Casting themselves down on the green, elastic, flower-sprinkled turf, they rolled one after the other down the smooth slopes of the terrace, the old "shepherd's steps," and by and by Johnnie, coming upon a patch of creeping thyme, rubbed his hands in the pale purple flowers, then rubbed her face to make it fragrant.

"Oh, 'tis sweet!" she cried. "Did 'ee ever see so many little flowers on the down? — 'tis as if they came out just for us." Then, indicating the tiny milkwort faintly sprinkling the turf all about them, "Oh, the little blue darlings! Did 'ee ever see such a dear blue?"

"Oh, aye, a prettier blue nor that," said Johnnie. "'Tis just here, Marty," and pressing her down he kissed her on the eyelids a dozen times.

"You silly Johnnie!"

"Be I silly, Marty? but I love the red too," and with that he kissed her on the mouth. "And, Marty, I do love the red on the breasties too — won't 'ee let me have just one kiss there?"

And she, to please him, opened her dress a little way, but blushingly, though she was his wife and nobody was there to see, but it seemed strange to her out of doors with the sun overhead. Oh, 'twas all delicious! Never was earth so heavenly sweet as on that wide green down, sprinkled with innumerable little flowers, under the wide blue sky and the all-illuminating sun that shone into their hearts!

At length, rising to her knees and looking up the green slope, she cried out: "Oh, Johnnie, there's the old thorn tree! Do 'ee remember when we played at crows on it and had such a fright? 'Twas the last time we came here together. Come, let's go to the old tree and see how it looks now."

Johnnie all at once became grave, and said No, he wouldn't go to it for anything. She was curious and made him tell her the reason. He had never forgotten that day and the fear that came into his mind on account of the words the strange man had spoken. She didn't know what the words were; she had been too frightened to listen, and so he had to tell her.

"Then, 'tis a wishing-tree for sure," Marty exclaimed. When he asked her what a wishing-tree was, she could only say that her old grandmother, now dead, had told her. 'Tis a tree that knows us and can do us good and harm, but will do good only to some; but they must go to it and ask for its protection, and they must offer it something as well as pray to it. It must be something bright — a little jewel or coloured bead is best, and if you haven't got such a thing, a bright-coloured ribbon, or strip of scarlet cloth or silk thread — which you must tie to one of the twigs.

"But we hurted the tree, Marty, and 'twill do no good to we."

They were both grave now; then a hopeful thought came to her aid. They had not hurt the tree intentionally; the tree knew that — it knew more than any human being. They might go and stand side by side under its branches and ask it to forgive them, and grant them all their desires. But they must not go empty-handed, they must have some bright thing with them when making their prayer. Then she had a fresh inspiration. She would take a lock of her own bright hair, and braid it with some of his, and tie it with a piece of scarlet thread.

Johnnie was pleased with this idea, and they agreed to take another Sunday afternoon walk and carry out their plan.

The projected walk was never taken, for by and by Marty's mother fell ill, and Marty had to be with her, nursing her night and day. And months went by, and at length, when her mother died, she was not in a fit condition to go long walks and climb those long, steep slopes. After the child was born, it was harder than ever to leave the house, and Johnnie, too, had so much work at the farm that he had little inclination to go out on Sundays. They ceased to speak of the tree, and their long-projected pilgrimage was impracticable until they could see better days. But the wished time never came, for, after the first child, Marty was never strong. Then a second child came, then a third; and so five years went by, of toil and suffering and love, and the tree, with all their hopes and fears and intentions regarding it, was less and less in their minds, and was all but forgotten. Only Johnnie, when at long intervals his master sent him to Salisbury with the cart, remembered it all only too well when, coming to the top of the down, he saw the old thorn directly before him. Passing it, he would turn his face away not to see it too closely, or, perhaps, to avoid being recognised by it. Then came the time of their extreme poverty, when there was no work at the farm and no one of their own people to help tide them over a season of scarcity, for the old people were dead or in the workhouse or so poor as to want help themselves. It was then that, in his misery at the sight of his ailing anxious wife — the dear Marty of the beautiful vanished days — and his three little hungry children, that he went out into the field one dark night to get them food.

 The whole sad history was in his mind as they slowly crawled up the hill, until it came to him that perhaps all their sufferings and this great disaster had been caused by the tree — by that something from the tree which had followed him, never resting in its mysterious enmity until it broke him. Was it too late to repair that terrible mistake? A gleam of hope shone on his darkened mind, and he made his passionate appeal to the constable. He had no offering — his hands were powerless now; but at least he could stand by it and touch it with his body and face and pray for its forgiveness, and for deliverance from the doom which threatened him. The constable had compassionately, or from some secret motive, granted his request; but alas! if in very truth the power he had come to believe in resided in the tree, he was too late in seeking it.

The trial was soon over; by pleading guilty Johnnie had made it a very simple matter for the court. The main thing was to sentence him. By an unhappy chance the judge was in one of his occasional bad moods; he had been entertained too well by one of the local magnates on the previous evening and had sat late, drinking too much wine, with the result that he had a bad liver, with a mind to match it. He was only too ready to seize the first opportunity that offered — and poor Johnnie's case was the first that morning — of exercising the awful power a barbarous law had put into his hands. When the prisoner's defender declared that this was a case which called loudly for mercy, the judge interrupted him to say that he was taking too much upon himself, that he was, in fact, instructing the judge in his duties, which was a piece of presumption on his part. The other was quick to make a humble apology and to bring his perfunctory address to a conclusion. The judge, in addressing the prisoner, said he had been unable to discover any extenuating circumstances in the case. The fact that he had a wife and family dependent on him only added to his turpitude, since it proved that no consideration could serve to deter him from a criminal act. Furthermore, in dealing with this case, he must take into account the prevalence of this particular form of crime; he would venture to say that it had been encouraged by an extreme leniency in many cases on the part of those whose sacred duty it was to administer the law of the land. A sterner and healthier spirit was called for at the present juncture. The time had come to make an example, and a more suitable case than the one now before him could not have been found for such a purpose. He would accordingly hold out no hope of a reprieve, but would counsel prisoner to make the best use of the short time remaining to him.

Johnnie standing in the dock appeared to the spectators to be in a half-dazed condition — as dull and spiritless a clodhopper as they had ever beheld. The judge and barristers, in their wigs and robes and gowns, were unlike any human beings he had ever looked on. He might have been transported to some other world, so strange did the whole scene appear to him. He only knew, or surmised, that all these important people were occupied in doing him to death, but the process, the meaning of their fine phrases, he could not follow. He looked at them, his glazed eyes travelling from face to face, to be fixed finally on the judge, in a vacant stare; but he scarcely saw them, he was all the time gazing on, and his mind occupied with, other forms and scenes invisible to the court. His village, his Marty, his dear little playmate of long ago, the sweet girl he had won, the wife and mother of his children, with her white, terrified face, clinging to him and crying in anguish: "Oh, Johnnie, what will they do to 'ee?" And all the time, with it all, he saw the vast green slope of the down, with the Salisbury road lying like a narrow white band across it, and close to it, near the summit, the solitary old tree.

During the delivery of the sentence, and when he was led from the dock and conveyed back to the prison, that image or vision was still present. He sat staring at the wall of his cell as he had stared at the judge, the fatal tree still before him. Never before had he seen it in that vivid way in which it appeared to him now, standing alone on the vast green down, under the wide sky, its four separate boles leaning a little way from each other, like the middle ribs of an open fan, holding up the widespread branches, the thin, open foliage, the green leaves stained with rusty brown and purple; and the ivy, rising like a slender black serpent of immense length, springing from the roots, winding upwards, and in and out, among the grey branches, binding them together, and resting its round, dark cluster of massed leaves on the topmost boughs. That green disc was the ivy-serpent's flat head and was the head of the whole tree, and there it had its eyes, which gazed for ever over the wide downs, watching all living things, cattle and sheep and birds and men in their comings and goings; and although fast-rooted in the earth, following them, too, in all their ways, even as it had followed him, to break him at last.

POSTSCRIPT

I
DEAD MAN'S PLACK

One of my literary friends, who has looked at the Dead Man's Plack in manuscript, has said by way of criticism that Elfrida's character is veiled. I am not to blame for that; for have I not already said, by implication at all events, in the Preamble, that my knowledge of her comes from outside. Something, or, more likely, *Somebody*, gave me her history, and it has occurred to me that this same Somebody was no such obscurity as, let us say, the Monk John of Glastonbury, who told the excavators just where to look for the buried chapel of Edgar, king and *saint*. I suspect that my informant was some one who knew more about Elfrida than any mere looker-on, monk or nun, and gossip-gatherer of her own distant day; and this suspicion or surmise was suggested by the following incident:

After haunting Dead Man's Plack, where I had my vision, I rambled in and about Wherwell on account of its association, and in one of the cottages in the village I became acquainted with an elderly widow, a woman in feeble health, but singularly attractive in her person and manner. Indeed, before making her acquaintance I had been informed by some of her relations and others in the place that she was not only the best person to seek information from, but was also the sweetest person in the village. She was a native born; her family had lived there for generations, and she was of that best South Hampshire type with an oval face, olive-brown skin, black eyes and hair, and that soft melancholy expression in the eyes common in Spanish women and not uncommon in the dark-skinned Hampshire women. She had been taught at the village school, and having attracted the attention and interest of the great lady of the place on account of her intelligence and pleasing manners, she was taken when quite young as lady's-maid, and in this employment continued for many years until her marriage to a villager.

One day, conversing with her, I said I had heard that the village was haunted by the ghost of a woman: was that true?

Yes, it was true, she returned.

Did she *know* that it was true? Had she actually seen the ghost?

Yes, she had seen it once. One day, when she was lady's-maid, she was in her bedroom, dressing or doing something, with another maid. The door was closed, and they were in a merry mood, talking and laughing, when suddenly they both at the same moment saw a woman with a still, white face walking through the room. She was in the middle of the room when they caught sight of her, and they both screamed and covered their faces with their hands. So great was her terror that she almost fainted; then in a few moments when they looked the apparition had vanished. As to the habit she was wearing, neither of them could say afterwards what it was like: only the white, still face remained fixed in their memory, but the figure was a dark one, like a dark shadow moving rapidly through the room.

If Elfrida then, albeit still in purgatory, is able to re-visit this scene of her early life and the site of that tragedy in the forest, it does not seem to me altogether improbable that she herself made the revelation I have written. And if this be so, it would account for the *veiled* character conveyed in the narrative. For even after ten centuries it may well be that all the coverings have not yet been removed, that although she has been dropping them one by one for ages, she has not yet come to the end of them. Until the very last covering, or veil, or mist is removed, it would be impossible for her to be absolutely sincere, to reveal her inmost soul with all that is most dreadful in it. But when that time comes, from the very moment of its coming she would cease automatically to be an exiled and tormented spirit.

If, then, Elfrida is herself responsible for the narrative, it is only natural that she does not appear in it quite as black as she has been painted. For the monkish chronicler was, we know, the Father of Lies, and so indeed in a measure are all historians and biographers, since they cannot see into hearts and motives or know all the circumstances of the case. And in this case they were painting the picture of their hated enemy and no doubt were not sparing in the use of the black pigment.

To know all is to forgive all, is a good saying, and enables us to see why even the worst among us can always find it possible to forgive himself.

II

AN OLD THORN

I was pleased at this opportunity of rescuing this story from a far-back number of the *English Review*, in which it first appeared, and putting it in a book. It may be a shock to the reader to be brought down from a story of a great king and queen of England in the tenth century to the obscure annals of a yokel and his wife who lived in a Wiltshire village only a century ago; or even less, since my poor yokel was hanged for sheep-stealing in 1821. But it is, I think, worth preserving, since it is the only narrative I know of dealing with that rare and curious subject, the survival of tree-worship in our own country. That, however, was not the reason of my being pleased.

It was just when I had finished writing the story of Elfrida that I happened to see in my morning paper a highly eulogistical paragraph about one of our long-dead and, I imagine, forgotten worthies. The occasion of the paragraph doesn't matter. The man eulogised was Mr. Justice Park — Sir James Allan Park, a highly successful barrister, who was judge from 1816 to his death in 1838. "As judge, though not eminent, he was sound, fair and sensible, a little irascible, but highly esteemed." He was also the author of a religious work. And that is all the particular Liar who wrote his biography in the D.N.B. can tell us about him.

It was the newspaper paragraph which reminded me that I had written about this same judge, giving my estimate of his character in my book, *A Shepherd's Life*, also that I was *thinking* about Park, the sound and fair and sensible judge, when I wrote "An Old Thorn." Here then, with apologies to the reader for quoting from my own book, I reproduce what

I wrote in 1905.

"From these memories of the old villagers I turn to the newspapers of the day to make a few citations.

"The law as it was did not distinguish between a case of the kind just related, of the starving, sorely-tempted Shergold, and that of the systematic thief: sheep-stealing was a capital offence and the man must be hanged, unless recommended to mercy, and we know what was meant by 'mercy' in those days. That so barbarous a law existed within memory of people to be found living in most villages appears almost incredible to us; but despite the recommendations to 'mercy' usual in a large majority of cases, the law of that time was not more horrible than the temper of the men who administered it. There are good and bad among all, and in all professions, but there is also a black spot in most, possibly all hearts, which may be developed to almost any extent, to change the justest, wisest, most moral men into 'human devils.' In reading the old reports and the expressions used by the judges in their summings-up and sentences, it is impossible not to believe that the awful power they possessed, and its constant exercise, had not only produced the inevitable hardening effect, but had made them cruel in the true sense of the word. Their pleasure in passing dreadful sentences was very thinly disguised by certain lofty conventional phrases as to the necessity of upholding the law, morality, and religion; they were, indeed, as familiar with the name of the Deity as any ranter in a conventicle, and the 'enormity of the crime' was an expression as constantly used in the case of the theft of a loaf of bread, or of an old coat left hanging on a hedge, by some ill-clad, half-starved wretch, as in cases of burglary, arson, rape, and murder.

"It is surprising to find how very few the real crimes were in those days, despite the misery of the people; that nearly all the 'crimes' for which men were sentenced to the gallows and to transportation for life, or for long terms, were offences which would now be sufficiently punished by a few weeks', or even a few days', imprisonment. Thus in April, 1825, I note that Mr. Justice Park commented on the heavy appearance of the calendar. It was not so much the number (170) of the offenders that excited his concern as it was the nature of the crimes with which they were charged. The worst crime in this instance was sheep-stealing!

"Again, this same Mr. Justice Park, at the Spring Assizes at Salisbury, 1827, said that though the calendar was a heavy one, he was happy to find, on looking at the depositions of the principal cases, that they were not of a very serious character. Nevertheless he passed sentence of death on twenty-eight persons, among them being one for stealing half a crown!

"Of the twenty-eight all but three were eventually reprieved, one of the fated three being a youth of 19, who was charged with stealing a mare and pleaded guilty in spite of a warning from the judge not to do so. This irritated the great man who had the power of life and death in his hand. In passing sentence the judge 'expatiated on the prevalence of the crime of horse-stealing and the necessity of making an example. The enormity of Read's crime rendered him a proper example, and he would therefore hold out no hope of mercy towards him.' As to the plea of guilty, he remarked that nowadays too many persons pleaded guilty, deluded with the hope that it would be taken into consideration and they would escape the severer penalty. He was determined to put a stop to that sort of thing; if Read had not pleaded guilty no doubt some extenuating circumstance would have come up during the trial and he would have saved his life.

"There, if ever, spoke the 'human devil' in a black cap!

"I find another case of a sentence of transportation for life on a youth of 18, named Edward Baker, for stealing a pocket-handkerchief. Had he pleaded guilty it might have been worse for him.

"At the Salisbury Spring Assizes, 1830, Mr. Justice Gazalee, addressing the grand jury, said that none of the crimes appeared to be marked with circumstances of great moral turpitude. The prisoners numbered 130; he passed sentences of death on twenty-nine, life transportations on five, fourteen years on five, seven years on eleven, and various terms of hard labour on the others." (A Shepherd's Life, pp. 241-4.)

Johnnie Budd was done to death before my principal informants, one 89 years old, the other 93, were born; but in their early years they knew the widow and her three children, and had known them and their children all their lives; thus the whole story of Johnnie and Marty was familiar to them. Now, when I thought of Johnnie's case and how he was treated at the trial, as it was told me by these old people, it struck me as so like that of the poor young man Read, who was hanged because he pleaded guilty, that I at once came to the belief that it was Mr. Justice Park who had tried him. I have accordingly searched the newspapers of that day, but have failed to find Johnnie's case. I can only suppose that this particular case was probably considered too unimportant to be reported at large in the newspapers of 1821. He was just one of a number convicted and sentenced to capital punishment.

When Johnnie was hanged his poor wife travelled to Salisbury and succeeded in getting permission to take the body back to the village for burial. How she in her poverty, with her three little children to keep, managed it I don't know. Probably some of the other poor villagers who pitied and perhaps loved her helped her to do it. She did even more: she had a grave-stone set above him with his name and the dates of his birth and death cut on it. And there it is now, within a dozen yards of the church door in the small old churchyard — the smallest village churchyard known to me; and Johnnie's and Marty's children's children are still living in the village.

FINIS

www.ingramcontent.com/pod-product-compliance
Lightning Source LLC
Chambersburg PA
CBHW020010050426
42450CB00005B/398